CGP

GCSE AQA

Business and Communication Systems

Answer Book

Contents

Published by CGP

ISBN: 978 1 84762 411 6

Groovy website: www.cgpbooks.co.uk
Printed by Elanders Ltd, Newcastle upon Tyne.

Based on the classic CGP style created by Richard Parsons.

The Answers

Section One — The Business Environment

Page 1 — Why Businesses Exist

Q1 Many possible answers, e.g.
Financial objectives:
1. Make a profit.
2. Maintain a reasonable income.
Non-financial objectives:
1. To provide the highest quality of customer service possible.
2. To limit the environmental damage caused by the business.

Q2 a) Most businesses will only pursue **non-financial** objectives if they will also **increase profits** in the long run.
 b) **Not-for-profit** organisations aim to make enough money to **cover their costs**. Any surplus is **put back into the business**.

Q3 Social enterprises aim to use their profits for the **benefit of society**, not to make the owners of the business wealthy.

Q4 b) and d) should be ticked.

Page 2 — Enterprise

Q1 a) True
 b) True
 c) False
 d) True
 e) True

Q2 A calculated risk means weighing up the **chances** of success and failure, considering the **consequences** of failure and then deciding if the risk is **worth taking**.

Q3 b) and e) should be ticked.

Q4 a) Jake identified a niche-market product that no company was providing but which people would be **willing to pay for**.
 b) Many possible answers, e.g.
 1. Initiative to seize opportunities.
 2. Drive and determination to turn ideas into practice.

Page 3 — Customers

Q1 a) A market-driven business would conduct market research to find out **what customers want**.
 b) If a firm focuses too much on developing a product and doesn't do enough market research, it may produce a product that there is **little demand for**.

Q2 a) should be ticked

Q3 a) **No** — the business should be able to give a date for dispatching products and **stick to it** more or less every time.

 b) **No** — 80% is a poor response rate. It suggests that the firm's telephone service is **unreliable** or that the company is not interested in responding to customers.

Q4 If customers are satisfied with the level of service they receive from a business, they are probably more likely to buy products again from the business in future (or recommend it to friends). These repeat purchases from loyal customers can bring in a lot of revenue without expensive advertising campaigns. **If the revenue increase is greater than the extra spending on improving customer service, then profits will rise.**

Page 4 — Stakeholders

Q1 A stakeholder is anyone who is affected by a business and what it does.

Q2 **Internal Stakeholders** — owners, directors, employees.
External Stakeholders — customers, suppliers, local community, government.

Q3 The firm's competitors will be affected if they start to **lose customers** to them.

Q4 a) **Local residents** are stakeholders — they may choose to not use Steve's pub because they are unhappy with the noise it creates. The music may **attract** some customers for the business. However, complaints about noise may be **investigated** by the local authorities.
 b) Customers are stakeholders — cheap prices keep **customers happy**, and attract new customers for the business. However, attracting more customers may cause more noise problems for local residents.
 c) Employees are stakeholders — good wages and lots of benefits will help keep the pub's **employees happy**. The business should benefit from **motivated** and **productive staff**, although paying high wages increases costs and may reduce the firm's profits. **Customers** may also benefit because happy staff may provide **better customer service**.

Page 5 — Measuring Business Success

Q1 Success criteria — The **targets** a business uses to measure whether or not it has met its objectives.
Strategy — The **way** that a business **coordinates the activities** of each department in order to try to achieve its objectives.

Q2 b) should be ticked.

Q3 a) A market share is the **percentage** of the total sales of the whole market that belong to a firm.

 b) 1. They will **lose sales** to the competitor.
 2. The competitor will have a **greater control** over the market.

Q4 Hints:
 • The main point here is that different stakeholders will have **different ideas of success** depending on their own individual interests.
 For example:
 • "The government are likely to believe that Durden's have had a successful year, because they have **employed 20 new staff** and **increased their takings** by 10% — if lots of businesses do well like this, the UK economy may grow. As a result, people may think that the government is doing a good job and vote for them in the next election."
 • "The shareholders of Durden's Soaps may have **mixed feelings** about the firm's success. They are likely to be **pleased by the increase in revenue**, but the **reduced profits** suggest that the firm's strategy may not have been quite right. These lower profits may mean that shareholders get a reduced payout in the form of a dividend."
 • "Consumers are likely to be **disappointed at the increase in prices**, but may feel that the company is **acting responsibly** by introducing its environmental policy."
 • "The local community will probably be **pleased that the pollution near the factory is being cleaned up**, and that **more jobs** are being created. However, they may feel the company's increased turnover has a downside if it means **more goods vehicles** will pass through the area."

Page 6 — Starting a New Business

Q1 b) and c) should be ticked.

Q2 Something that makes a product **different** to competitors' products and is **valued** by customers.

Q3 a) Adding value means making a product that customers will **pay more** for than it's cost the business to produce.
 b) Products that are made to a **high quality** and with a **good appearance** are **more desirable** to own, so customers are willing to pay more for them.
 c) A good brand image can help a product become **well known** and **trusted** — people are happy to buy products from a company they trust even if they cost a little bit extra.

The Answers

Q4 Customers may be willing to pay extra for the **convenience** of having pasta that cooks more quickly.

Page 7 — Marketing and Market Research

Q1 a) and d) should be ticked.

Q2 The **needs and wants** of customers can **change over time**. A firm's marketing mix needs to reflect these changes, or they will become **out-of-date** and **lose sales**.

Q3 b), d) and e) should be ticked.

Q4 a) Quantitative
b) Qualitative
c) Secondary

Q5 Qualitative data is about things that **can't** be turned into **numbers**, like people's opinions. This makes it hard to compare different pieces of data or draw graphs or charts which would help you spot any patterns in your data.

Page 8 — Analysing the Market

Q1 a) A market segment is a **group of people** within the market who have **something in common**.
b) E.g. age, gender, location, social class, religion.

Q2 a) A **need or want** among some customers in the market that's **not being met** by competing businesses.
b) If a firm can identify areas where its competitors are **weak**, it can try to do **those things better**. This may attract **more customers** to the firm, increasing its market share. If a firm tries to compete with other firms' **strengths**, it's **less likely** to succeed.

Q3 a) This gives the business an idea of **how much** customers are **prepared to pay** for a product, so they can price their product realistically.
b) The business may be able to launch 'budget' products at **lower prices**, or 'luxury' products at **higher prices**.

Q4 Many possible answers, e.g.
The profit figures are low in January, steadily increase towards June, July and August, and fall again towards December.
To increase their profits during the winter, Crazy Juice could change their **marketing mix** during these months. They could increase **promotion** of their products or the **price** of the juice could be lowered to increase sales. They could also launch a new 'warm juice' **product** because there is likely to be greater demand for warm drinks during the winter.

Section Two — Administration & Organisation

Page 9 — Organisational Structure

Q1 **Supervisor** — Looking after specific projects or small teams of operatives.
Manager — Responsible for organising the activities involved in carrying out the firm's strategy.
Operative — Not responsible for any other workers. Given specific tasks to complete.
Director — Decides the firm's strategy and targets.

Q2 a) Tall Hierarchy:
Effect on communication — communication up and down the hierarchy can be slow and messages may get distorted.
b) Circular chart:
Effect on communication — communication between senior managers and operatives may improve because the structure is designed so that nobody feels they are at the bottom.
c) Flat hierarchy:
Effect on communication — communication is quick and efficient, although managers may get overwhelmed if they are in charge of too many people.
d) Matrix structure:
Effect on communication — can lead to operatives being given conflicting tasks by different managers.

Q3 You could use a word processor for this task, but it's probably not the best software for the job. A **desktop publishing** package would be better — it's easier to move objects around the page and line them up. The example below was made using the text and shape tools in a **graphics package**.

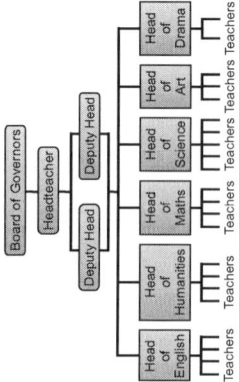

Page 10 — Administration in Business

Q1 a) disseminating
b) storing
c) disseminating
d) retrieving
e) processing

Q2 a) If a customer's details can be retrieved **quickly** and **accurately**, it means that their queries can be dealt with more quickly.
b) Many possible answers, e.g.
1. Sales data can be **processed** to look at how the business is performing compared to competitors — this can help show areas of the business that need improving.
2. Good administration means that a firm can complete tasks **more quickly** and use **fewer resources**. This will **reduce** the firm's **costs**, and mean that it can **reduce** its **prices** compared to the prices of its **competitors**.

Q3 Many possible answers, e.g.
a) A business could use this information to keep track of its **energy efficiency**. If the bills become too high, they could look into ways of improving their energy efficiency.
b) A firm could use this to measure the **success** of the advertising campaign by comparing the amount of money they spent to the amount they made from extra sales.

Page 11 — Routine & Non-Routine Tasks

Q1 a) True
b) False
c) False

Q2 The following should be ticked: replacing an ink cartridge in a printer; changing the till roll at a cashier's desk; inputting phone numbers onto a database.

Q3 It's a task that requires a mixture of **creativity** and **expert knowledge** and can only be successfully completed by **experienced** staff with technical expertise.

Q4 a) **Restaurant manager** — the choice of head chef will have a major effect on the quality of the restaurant's food. This is a non-routine decision, which should be made by somebody with business experience and responsibility.
b) **Chef** — since it's a decision that requires some amount of specialist skill and experience, the chef has the most expertise to make this decision.

The Answers

Page 12 — Planning

Q1 Planning — Thinking about what needs to be achieved and working out the best way to do it with the resources available.
Prioritising — Deciding which tasks are most important and dealing with them sooner.

Q2 a) True
b) False
c) False
d) True

Q3 a) Projects may fall **behind schedule** and end up being **completed late** if insufficient time has been allowed for tasks, or they are not being done in an efficient way.
b) Poor planning might result in more **materials** and **resources** being **wasted**, so the project may end up costing more than it should.
c) Poor planning might result in **errors** being made in the project. Also, if time planning has been poor, staff may feel pressurised into **cutting corners** in order to meet deadlines.

Q4 a) This helps managers to **prioritise** the tasks so that the most important ones are completed first.
b) Milestones help managers to **track the progress** of a project and to check that it is on schedule.
c) Access to information about similar past projects helps planning because managers can see **what worked well** in the past and **what problems may arise**.

Page 13 — Efficient Use of Resources

Q1 a) should be ticked.

Q2 E.g. **Option A** is the most suitable because it's an appropriate size for the firm. The offices are in a new development, so they may be able to expand further in the future. Option B is too large for the firm — money would be wasted heating the open plan office, most of which wouldn't be occupied.

Q3 b) should be ticked.

Q4 Using resources more efficiently means that there will be **less waste**, and **less pollution**. Being energy efficient can reduce the amount of pollution from fossil fuels, which is contributing to climate change.

Q5 Your memo should be laid out in the standard format. So you'll need:
• A **heading** saying 'Memo' or 'Memorandum'.
• Four lines saying who the memo is **to**, who it's **from**, the **date** and the **subject** (or **re:**).

• You should write the main text of the memo underneath these. Remember that it's a **formal** business document, so use formal English. But bear in mind that you're trying to **persuade** and **reassure** the staff, so try to be **sympathetic** to their concerns.
Here are some points you could include in your memo:
• Buying cheaper computers might be better in the **short term** as it will save money, but they will probably need **upgrading** sooner — this would be costly for the firm.
• Compared with better quality computers, cheaper computers might become **slow** and hard to use quickly — this will reduce the **efficiency** of the business and could affect customer service.
• Some employees have expressed concern about job losses if the firm spends too much money. But the business will suffer more in the long term if they lose customers due to inefficient resources.
• Better quality computers will be faster and more powerful, which should make staff's jobs easier and less frustrating.

Page 14 — Office Layout

Q1 Open plan offices:
Main features — large space containing many desks.
Advantage — e.g. it can improve communication as staff are sat together, so can quickly share ideas, ask questions etc.
Disadvantage — e.g. with lots of people in one office it can be noisy, which can affect concentration — the quality and quantity of an employee's work could be reduced.
Cellular offices:
Main features — space is divided up into small rooms with solid walls. Rooms are used by a few workers or just one person.
Advantage — e.g. staff have quiet and privacy. This is useful if they need to concentrate.
Disadvantage — e.g. it can make supervision of junior staff more difficult — they may not get all the support they need.

Q2 a) **Open plan office** — it will be easier for the members of each team to discuss ideas with each other.
b) **Cellular office** — staff will be able to talk to clients in privacy about difficult matters.

Q3 a) It means that something has been designed to be **comfortable** and **easy to use**, with less physical effort required.

b) The more comfortable staff are, the more **motivated** and **productive** they will be. Ergonomically designed furniture can also help **reduce health problems** and injuries, e.g. tiredness, back pain, eye strain — this may reduce the amount of time staff are off work with illnesses, **saving** the company **money**.

Page 15 — Modern Working Practices

Q1 a) Flexitime is when workers can **choose their weekly hours**, provided they work during the firm's core hours. Flexitime can make it **harder to monitor** staff's work, so the **quality and quantity** of their work may fall.
b) i) Teleworking is when staff **work from home**, e.g. using the internet to connect to their office.
ii) Many possible answers, e.g. **Benefit:** They will spend less time commuting to work. **Drawback:** With reduced personal contact, workers might feel lonely and may not receive the support they need.

Q2 Hot-desking means that employees don't have their own special desk — they use **any free desk** in the office instead. It will offer flexibility for Creativ-Ads by allowing them to move staff around when project teams change so that teams can **communicate more easily**.

Q3 a) Using ICT to connect people in different locations using sound and/or video.
b) It is **cheaper** to hold a teleconference than to pay for the managers to travel to the different offices. It is also **less time consuming** — travelling to other offices means managers spend a lot of time out of the office. With teleconferencing, they're only unavailable for the actual length of the meeting.
c) Many possible answers, e.g.
1. It can be **expensive** to buy and use the technology.
2. It can be **impersonal** — it may be harder to build up good relationships over a video-link.

Page 16 — Health and Safety at Work

Q1 Employees should:
1. Act responsibly
2. Carry out tasks as they've been trained to do.
3. Report any dangerous practices.

The Answers

Q2 The records in the accident book can help firms to **identify hazards** — this information can be used to help **prevent future accidents** by informing staff of potential hazards or making changes to the workplace.

Q3 Many possible answers, e.g.
1. Repetitive strain injury.
2. Eye strain.
3. Circulation problems.

Q4 Hints:
- Presentation slides should only contain a **small amount** of information — the details should be given in the talk. Use **short bullet points** to summarise the main points, and make sure the text is **large enough** to read from a **distance**.
- Diagrams can help, too — try to include some charts or illustrations to help explain the information (e.g. a picture showing how to sit at a desk with good posture).
- If you're using **presentation software**, you can include effects like **animations** and **transitions** to liven up your slides. Use these sparingly — too many can be distracting (and some of them don't look very professional).

Ideas that could be covered on the slides:
- Take regular breaks from computers, e.g. taking a walk.
- Exercise your fingers and hands regularly.
- Make sure you have good posture at your desk to avoid back strain.
- Employers should provide correct equipment, e.g. ergonomically-designed keyboards, chairs and desks, and monitors that can be adjusted.
- Make sure there are no loose cables around and there are clear walkways around the office.

Section Three — ICT Data Systems

Page 17 — Data Processing Systems

Q1 **Primary data** is **collected first-hand** by the business itself whereas **secondary data** is information that has been **collected** by someone **outside the firm**.

Q2 Many possible answers, e.g.
Benefits:
1. Useful for when hard copies of documents are needed.
2. Doesn't require expensive computer equipment to be purchased.

Drawbacks:
1. Paper documents can take up a lot of storage space.
2. It can take a long time to process data as it has to all be done by hand.

Q3 b) and d) should be ticked.

Q4 Hardware — The physical parts of a computer system
Software — Programs that can be used on computers

Q5
a) Hardware
b) Hardware
c) Software
d) Software

Page 18 — Computers and Input Devices

Q1 a), b) and d) should be ticked.

Q2 A laptop is more **portable** than a desktop computer, so she can carry it with her, do all of her work on the **same machine** and work while she **travels**, e.g. on trains.

Q3 A computer network is a number of computers **connected** together so they can communicate with each other.

Q4
a) An input device is any **hardware** that can be used to **enter data** onto a computer system.
b) A QWERTY keyboard has many keys, most of which have an individual letter or number on them, while a concept keyboard has a symbol or word on each key which represents a piece of data stored in the computer, e.g. a product's price.
c) Situations where the **same data** needs entering **over and over again**, e.g. in shops and restaurants.
d) Prolonged use may lead to **repetitive strain injury** (RSI).

Q5 More than one possible answer, e.g.
Benefit: It's more **intuitive** than using just a keyboard and can also be quicker.
Drawback: Can cause **RSI** if used for long periods.

Page 19 — More Input Devices

Q1 Sam can take **pictures** of the clothes to put on his website — people will be **more likely to buy his products** if they can actually see them.

Q2
a) Scanners take digital images of documents.
b) OCR software takes the scanned image of a document and turns any text in the image into text that can be **edited** using word-processing software.

Q3
a) Electronic Point of Sale
b) EPOS devices have a **computer system** linked to a **scanner** which reads **bar codes** on products. The bar code identifies an individual product and the computer system retrieves stored data about that product. They can be used to automatically add up the prices of items at a shop checkout and adjust stock records.

Q4 He could use a voice-recognition system which could convert his speech into text or commands for the computer.

Q5
a) E.g. when a customer buys an item online and enters their details.
b) Customers enter the information **themselves**, so can check that their own details are correct. Many electronic forms also use **validation checks** to prevent customers from accidentally entering inaccurate data. Paper forms will have to be copied onto a computer at some point to store the data and **mistakes** can be made, e.g. if handwriting is unclear.

Page 20 — Data Storage

Q1 Internal storage devices are built into a computer, whereas external storage devices can be removed from the computer.

Q2
a) gigabytes
b) It means that **everyone knows** where data is stored (and can **easily access** it if they have permission). It also makes it **easier to back up the data**, since it's all stored in one place.
c) If a hard drive fails then all the data on it may be lost — this can cause major problems for a business. Backing up data means that if this does happen there will still be a copy of all the data.

Q3 To **transfer** files between different computers.

Q4 Many possible answers, e.g.
They are **portable**, and can be connected to many different electronic devices, e.g. desktop computers, laptops, PDAs, mobile phones and digital cameras. It is also **much quicker** to transfer data between devices using a memory card or USB stick than it is using CDs or DVDs.

Q5
1. They are **easily lost**, so confidential information or important details may fall into the wrong hands.
2. They can **transfer viruses** onto the firm's network if an employee uses the same USB stick at both home and work and has a virus on their home computer.

The Answers

Page 21 — Data Storage and Back-Up

Q1 CD-ROM — Read only disks. Often used by manufacturers to distribute their software.
CD-R — Sold as blank disks. Data can be recorded onto them once.
CD-RW — Sold as blank disks. Data can be written onto them and deleted many times.

Q2 a), b) and d) should be ticked

Q3 Many possible answers, e.g.
1. It takes a **long time** to write data onto them.
2. They can be **easily scratched or damaged**, which can make the data on them unreadable.

Q4 **Advantage:** Cheap way to store a large amount of data.
Disadvantage: Accessing data on a magnetic tape can be slow.

Q5 Web-based storage is where data is **uploaded to the internet** and downloaded again when it's needed. It is remote storage because the data is stored in a **separate place** from the computer that uses the data.

Q6 In case the building is burgled or damaged by fire. Otherwise the firm would lose both the data and the back-ups.

Page 22 — Output Devices — Printers

Q1 An output device is a piece of **hardware** that is used to **communicate the results** of data processing.

Q2 Sometimes firms need a **hard copy** of a document for their **reference**, or as a **permanent record**. It might also be the best way to communicate with customers, other employees etc.

Q3 Many possible answers, e.g.
Advantages:
1. They print high quality documents.
2. They're fast — usually over 10 pages per minute (ppm).
Disadvantages:
1. They can be quite expensive.
2. They contain a lot of complex equipment — so they're expensive to repair.

Q4 1. They can **print onto rolls** of paper which don't need replacing often.
2. They are very **reliable**, so won't often break while people are queuing at tills.

Q5 a) and c) should be ticked.

Q6 Hints:
• From the information you're given in the question, it seems that a laser printer would be the best choice. But you need to say **why**.

• E.g. Duncan should buy a laser printer. They are fast and relatively cheap to run. This makes them suitable for printing the large quantities of documents that Duncan will be printing. They are ideal for use on a network like Duncan has in his office because they print documents quickly. One drawback is that they are quite expensive to buy but in this case Duncan and his colleagues will be using the printer a lot, so the cost will be justified.

Page 23 — More Output Devices

Q1 a) The graphic designer's screen will probably be **larger** with a **higher resolution** — an operative could do their work on a smaller screen with lower resolution.
b) LCD monitors are **lighter** and they **take up less space** on desks than cathode-ray tube monitors. They can be **moved around more easily** and allow desk space to be used more efficiently. They also **use less power** than cathode-ray monitors.

Q2 a) LCD projector.
b) The projector can be connected to a computer and used to project whatever is on the computer monitor onto a large screen.
c) Many possible answers, e.g.
1. It needs a screen and dimly lit conditions to get the best image.
2. It can be expensive to buy the projector and the computer equipment to connect to it.

Q3 a) Speakers
b) Monitor
c) Printer
d) LCD projector
e) Headphones

Page 24 — Keeping Data Secure

Q1 Many possible answers, e.g.
1. If the company holds data about customers, it is **required by law** to keep the data secure and can face **heavy fines** if it doesn't.
2. Some data could **reduce a firm's competitiveness** if it leaked out to competitors.
3. Data that's been **corrupted** or altered by unauthorised users is **useless** to a business.

Q2 a) Keep equipment in a **locked, alarmed** building.
b) So that only **authorised** people have access to the computer network.

c) i) By **monitoring all the traffic** coming into the network and **denying access** to any unauthorised users.
ii) Screensavers can be set up so that a **password** is needed before the computer can be used again. This stops an unauthorised user from accessing someone's computer when they are away from their desk.

Q3 a) Anti-virus software
b) Anti-spyware software
c) Anti-adware software
d) Anti-spam software

Page 25 — Data Protection and the Law

Q1 b) and d) should be ticked.

Q2 a) She would be allowed to see this information **at any time**, provided she gives **notice** (and possibly pays a small fee).
b) **Yes**, Murray's Motors can do this if the customer has **given permission** for their data to be used this way.
c) This data is **not relevant** to the purchase of a car, so it's illegal to store it.
d) This is **not legal** — they are breaking the principle that says that **data should be properly disposed of**. Anybody could take the CDs from the skip and have access to customers' financial details.

Q3 a) A data subject is a person whose personal data is stored by a business or other organisation.
b) Possible answers:
1. The right to **view** their personal data (although they may have to pay a fee).
2. The right to prevent data from being processed if it may be **damaging** or **distressing** to them.
3. The right to **compensation** if they are damaged or distressed by processed data.
4. The right to have **inaccurate** data **corrected** or **deleted**.
5. The right to prevent data being used to send them **junk mail**.

Section Four — Human Resources

Page 26 — Patterns of Work

Q1 a) True
b) True
c) True
d) True
e) False

The Answers

Q2 a) A permanent contract of employment has no **end date**.
  b) Temporary workers will find it **harder** to get a mortgage than permanent workers.
  c) A temporary contract is for a **fixed period**.

Q3 Employing temporary workers means it is **easier** for the firm to **adjust the number of staff** employed, without having to make workers **redundant** (which costs the firm money and is bad for morale).

Q4 Many possible answers, e.g. Job title, start date, hours of work, payment details, location of employment, holiday allowance, disciplinary procedure and the length of notice to be given if an employee wants to leave.

Q5 Hints:
  • You could start your answer by giving a **definition** of permanent and temporary contracts.
  • Then talk about the **advantages** and **disadvantages** of **both** types of contract to **Abby** — not the employer.
  • E.g. "Abby could benefit from temporary work because the **wages** might be higher than if she was in a permanent position. As the work is temporary she could also choose when she works, e.g. she could have a break after the end of one contract before she accepts another. Her employer might offer her the chance to **renew** her contract after the end date, if she wants to make her employment more continuous, but there would be no guarantee of this. Abby may find it more difficult to get loans or a mortgage because banks will see her as more of a risk. Also, she wouldn't receive any **redundancy** money (which she would do if made redundant from a permanent position)."

Page 27 — Recruitment — Job Analysis

Q1 A job description contains information on **what the job is** and its main **purpose** and **duties**. It will also include details on who the candidate would **report to** and any **responsibilities** they will have. A person specification refers to the actual **qualifications**, **experience**, **skills** and **personal qualities** that the candidate will need for the job.

Q2 **Job description** headings: Job title, Reports to, Responsible for, Duties, Main purpose of job. **Person specification** headings: Desirable qualities, Essential qualities, Qualifications, Skills, Attitudes, Experience.

Q3 a) Many possible answers, e.g. Description of role, rate of pay, location of job (i.e. which department), what training is offered, what additional benefits are offered.
  b) Many possible answers, e.g. **Advantage:** It's cheaper advertising the post internally, e.g. on a notice board, compared with advertising externally, e.g. in a newspaper. **Disadvantage**: The promotion would leave another vacancy to fill within the business.

Page 28 — Recruitment — The Selection Process

Q1 Possible answers: personal details, skills, qualifications, work experience, hobbies and interests, referees.

Q2 a) A **large business** is likely to have **many applications** to read. Using application forms means the firm can get just the information it wants, and doesn't have to filter out the irrelevant information which may be included in other forms of application.
  b) E.g. A good application will refer to the **skills** and **qualities** mentioned in the **job description** and **person specification**. The information will also be well written, accurate and to the point.

Q3 a) The employer will read each candidate's CV and application form and **compare** the information on these to the job description and person specification. This allows them to decide which candidates have the best skills, qualifications and qualities for the job — these people will be put on a short-list.
  b) Many possible answers, e.g. **Advantage**: An interview allows the employer to test a candidate's **verbal skills** and **confidence** — these can't be seen on a written application. **Disadvantage**: People often **don't behave naturally** in a formal interview. Also, the skills needed for doing well at interview are often **different** from the skills needed for the job.

Q4 Hints:
  • Your letter should follow the standard business letter format using **fully-blocked style** and **open punctuation**.
  • Remember to include the **sender's address**, the **receiver's address**, the **date**, a **greeting line**, the **main text** (including the date and time of the interview), a **closing line** and the **name** and **position** of the sender.

  • Insert **merge fields** that link to the appropriate columns of the spreadsheet — you should end up with eight different letters.

Page 29 — Employment Law

Q1 The company's discipline procedure.

Q2 Age, sex, race, religion, disability, sexual orientation.

Q3 a) **No**
  b) It is only legal to dismiss staff for **incompetence** or **gross misconduct**. A single accident is not a good enough reason.

Q4 If the job they were doing **no longer exists**.

Q5 They could appeal to an **industrial tribunal**. They may be **compensated** or **reinstated** to their job.

Q6 It can be **expensive** and **time-consuming** to keep up with new legislation. Firms may find themselves going through costly court cases to prove that they've behaved legally — if they haven't, they may be fined.

Page 30 — Staff Training

Q1 a) At the **start** of a worker's employment.
  b) To **welcome** the employee, **introduce** them to other staff and **explain company rules** as well as initial training on **how to do their job**.

Q2 Advantage: Trainee staff can still be **productive** while they're learning the job. Disadvantage: Trainees may **pick up bad working habits** from existing staff.

Q3 a) **External** training.
  b) The staff at the university are likely to be better qualified in training.
  c) Paying for external courses may be **very expensive**, and Silkisoft may also have to pay employees' **travelling costs**.

Q4 Many possible answers, e.g. Benefits of training to employers:
  1. Trained staff should be better at their jobs and therefore **more efficient** and **productive**.
  2. Training staff can give them the **skills to do new jobs** within the firm — this can **save time** and **money** on advertising jobs externally.
  3. Staff may feel like they're **progressing** in the firm and so **stay with the firm** for longer — **reducing recruitment costs**.
  Benefits of training to employees:
  1. Employees with up-to-date knowledge and skills should be able to do their jobs better — which can increase **job satisfaction** and **motivation**.
  2. Over time, gaining new skills may lead to **promotions** with **better pay** and **more responsibility**.

The Answers

3.   It can **improve job prospects** — it may help staff to get better jobs with other firms and achieve their career ambitions.

Page 31 — Financial Rewards

Q1   a)   A wage **changes** depending on the amount of work done by an employee. A salary is a **fixed** amount paid every month.

b)   **Advantage:** The business knows how much it is paying out every month.
Disadvantage: The salary isn't directly linked to performance so it doesn't encourage employees to work harder to earn more money.

Q2   a)   Train driver
Method of payment: **time rate**
Explanation: It is difficult to measure the output of a train driver, but easy to record the amount of time worked.

b)   Textiles worker
Method of payment: **piece rate**
Explanation: The worker can be paid according to the number of cushions they produce. This will motivate them to be productive.

c)   Double-glazing salesperson
Method of payment: **commission**
Explanation: The worker will receive a basic salary, and earn extra money for every sale they make. This will motivate them to make more sales.

Q3   **Commission** is an **additional payment** made to sales workers to 'top-up' their salary. They get a payment **for each item they sell**. A **bonus** is a **lump sum** that is paid in addition to a worker's normal salary **for performing well**, e.g. if they've met all their targets. Bonuses are usually paid once a year.

Q4   An overtime rate is what is paid to workers for **extra hours** worked on top of their normal working week. This rate is usually more than their normal rate of pay.

Page 32 — Financial Rewards

Q1   Gross pay is the amount of money an employee is paid, e.g. their wage or salary. The net pay is what the worker actually gets to keep after deductions from their gross pay, e.g. tax, national insurance.

Q2   1% of £1240 = £1240/100 = £12.40
So 5% of £1240 = £12.40 × 5
= £62 per month

Q3   1% of £9 = £9/100 = £0.09
So 3% of £9 = £0.09 × 3 = £0.27
So the new hourly wage is £9 + £0.27
= £9.27 per hour

Q4   a)   A fringe benefit is an **extra perk** given to staff in addition to their pay as an extra **incentive** to work hard.

b)   The staff benefit because they get goods cheaper and so can save money. It's good for the firm as they will sell more products and their staff won't be buying similar products from their competitors.

Q5   Hints:
*   There are plenty of fringe benefits you could choose to include on your poster. For example: staff discount, a pension scheme, life insurance, private medical insurance, a meal allowance, gym membership.
*   **Graphics software** or **desktop publishing software** are usually the best options for making posters — it's easy to **combine** text and graphics in these packages.
*   Posters are usually quite **visual**, so use appropriate **graphics** (e.g. photos or clip art) to illustrate the benefits you're talking about.
*   Make sure the text is **striking** and easy to read, and don't go into loads of detail about each benefit. A poster is supposed to **catch people's attention** — they can find out more afterwards if they're interested.

Section Five — Communication

Page 33 — Purposes of Communication

Q1   Feedback is a **response** given back to the **sender** of a message. It shows that the receiver has **got** the message and **understood** it — and can be used to judge how successful the communication has been. Feedback can be written, verbal or visual.

Q2   a)   **No** — you only know that Barry has been sent a message, you can't tell he has read it.

b)   He may get a **reply** (feedback) from Barry to say whether it's possible for the meeting to be moved to 3pm.

Q3   **Written:** information can be kept and re-read — this is useful for complex information.
Oral: this is a more personal form of communication and is good for getting immediate feedback.
Visual: these are good for expressing meaning quickly without words, e.g. graphical methods can be used to show data and technical methods clearly.

Q4   E.g. I think that Cliff should use a **written** method of communication, as this is a more formal way of explaining the situation and apologising. His message is fairly **urgent**, as the event was due to be next week, so he should use a medium that is likely to get to the customer quickly such as **email** or a **letter** posted **first class**.

Page 34 — Internal and External Communication

Q1   **Internal** communication happens between people **inside a firm** and **external** communication happens with people **outside a firm**.

Q2   a)   External
b)   Internal
c)   External

Q3   Staff will be **better informed** about what is going on in the firm which can **improve motivation** and **productivity**. Good communication between **staff** also means that they should **work together better** and make **fewer mistakes**.

Q4   Many possible answers, e.g.
1.   **Adverts** — these remind customers about a firm's products or inform them about new products.
2.   **Market research** — this can reveal the wants and needs of customers so firms can identify gaps in the market for products or services.

Q5   a)   It can help **reduce** the number of **misunderstandings** — so orders are correct and arrive on time. The firm may also be able to build up a **relationship** with their suppliers, which may allow them to **negotiate discounts** etc.

b)   The customer is **less likely** to be **annoyed** if they have been told in advance that a delivery will be late. This means they are **less likely** to **avoid** using the company in future, or tell family and friends not to use the company.

Page 35 — Barriers to Communication

Q1   a)   Many possible answers, e.g.
1.   Use of **jargon**, e.g. Energy Saver 2000 — a non-Leccy customer wouldn't know what this means.
2.   **Visual noise** — the page contains lots of information, all close together, making it hard to read.

b)   These problems will make the letter **hard to read** and **understand**. Rather than attracting customers, the reader may **lose interest** when reading the letter and therefore choose not to switch to Leccy.

The Answers

Q2 The feelings and opinions of people can affect how they communicate — if colleagues find they often **disagree** or **don't get on** personally, then messages may be **misunderstood**. A lack of **personal trust** between colleagues can also affect how people **react** to messages (e.g. they may feel that messages from that person are likely to be **unfair** in some way).

Q3 a) 1. If the train is **noisy** she may find it hard to hear what her clients/ co-workers are saying.
2. She may keep **losing phone signal**.
b) The clients might get **annoyed** and **frustrated** at the poor communication — this will give them a **negative impression** of Anna's firm and make them **less likely to do business** with the firm.

Q4 a) It can **avoid embarrassment** for the firm and **confusion** for the customers. Lots of mistakes would create an **unprofessional image** — customers may **lose trust** and decide to use a different company instead. It's also **illegal** to **incorrectly advertise** or label a product.
b) Spelling errors:
recieved — received
electricty — electricity
definitly — definitely
experiance — experience
there — their

Page 36 — Written Communication — Letters

Q1 The changes might be **complicated** so it's useful for the customer to have a written copy of them to **refer** back to. It also acts as a **permanent record** of the communication for both the bank and the customer.

Q2 a) The message is **urgent** — the letter may not get delivered in time or could get lost in the post. The sender will also have to wait to get feedback about whether the message has been received and understood.
b) Many possible answers, e.g.
Email — the colleague will receive the email much quicker than by post, giving them the opportunity to respond.

Q3 The letter to the person who made the booking will be quite **formal**, clearly stating a booking has been made and including important information.
The letter to the girl will be much more **informal** and **chatty** — Cheryl will want to create a fun, friendly image of the firm so that the girl looks forward to the day.

Q4 It means that information is presented in a **clear** and **uncomplicated** way, so the reader is much more **likely** to **understand** the communication. It also gives the business a **professional** image.

Q5 Letters that are not sent using a special delivery service may get **lost** or **stolen** in the post.

Page 37 — Internal Written Communication

Q1 a) Memos are **formal written messages** that are sent to people **inside an organisation**. They're often used to remind or update staff about something, e.g. a policy, an event.
b) **Advantage:** A permanent record of the message can be kept to prove the message was sent to staff. **Disadvantage:** There's no guarantee that staff will actually read the message.
c) E-mails are **much quicker** and they don't use any paper — which can **save money** and make the company more **environmentally friendly**.

Q2 The report will give **detailed advice** on the ways to reduce the warehouse costs — this information is not directly **relevant to customers**. The report will probably also contain information that the business doesn't want anyone outside the company to read.

Q3 Many possible answers, e.g.
1. It can stay on display for a **long time** — giving all members of staff the **opportunity** to see it.
2. It's **cheaper** to make one notice for the notice board than lots of copies to send to every member of staff.

Q4 It's a large company so a newsletter would be a good way to **inform** staff about **events** and changes within the company. If staff are well informed it can improve **motivation** and **productivity**. It may also help them feel more like part of a team. However it will be **expensive** as the newsletter will have to go out to all 300 staff.

Page 38 — More Written Communication

Q1 Catalogues usually give **details about products**. But like all communication, catalogues can help a firm create a certain **image** for itself, which can help it appeal to its target markets. For example, a '**fancy**' catalogue with glossy pages and lots of attractive photos might give an impression of **luxury** products, while a **quirky**, unusual catalogue might appeal to a different group of customers.

Q2 a) A **brochure** would be most appropriate because the firm wants to publicise a new range of products, and will probably want to include more detail than they could fit onto a flyer.
b) A **flyer** would be most appropriate because the shop only wants to communicate a simple message i.e. "get free delivery on all orders in February" and wants to do it in an eye-catching way.

Q3 a) Invoices are used as a **written request for payment** from the customer.
b) It makes it easier to **track** what orders have been made and what payments are due from clients.

Q4 a) It helps the firm to see whether the candidate has the **right skills** and **qualifications** needed for the job and to decide whether to offer the candidate an interview.
b) It's important to check for **good spelling, punctuation** and **grammar** to make sure their CV **reads well**. If there are any mistakes, the candidate won't make a **good first impression** on the employer.

Q5 Hints:
- CVs usually just contain **text**, so a **word processor** would be ideal for this task.
- Remember to break up your CV into clear **sections**. For example:
  1. Your **name** and **contact details**.
  2. **Employment history** — include details of any part-time jobs you've had outside school, in date order.
  3. **Education** — list the details of all the schools you've attended, in date order.
  4. **Qualifications** — you could use your predicted GCSE grades here.
  5. **Hobbies and interests**. If you've got certificates for sports, music etc., you could list them here.
- Keep your details **brief** and **accurate** — you're trying to give a good impression, so check your spelling, punctuation and grammar, and make sure all your facts are right.
- Don't use loads of fancy formatting. Stick to **black text** (it's easier to photocopy), and make sure the section headings are clear.

The Answers

Page 39 — Electronic Communication

Q1 a) Faxed documents are usually **lower quality** than the original, and it is **cheaper** and **quicker** to use email than send a fax. Also, nearly all businesses will have a computer connected to the internet on which they can receive emails. However, **fewer and fewer businesses are likely to have a fax machine** as this medium becomes less popular, meaning the number of people able to receive faxed documents will decrease.

b) Hand-written notes can be turned into a **computer file** using a **scanner**, and then sent by **email**.

Q2 Many possible answers, e.g.
Advantages:
1. Emails can be sent all over the world within a few seconds.
2. Copies of the same email can be sent to lots of people.
3. It's cheaper to send an email than use many other forms of communication.
Disadvantages:
1. Both the sender and receiver need access to a computer and the internet.
2. They're less formal than letters so they may not be appropriate for sending all messages.
3. They're not always very confidential — other people might be able to get access to them.

Q3 a) Many possible answers, e.g.
1. By leaving a message on a **guestbook**.
2. By completing a **form** which is sent to the firm as an email.

b) They could **password-protect** these parts — users will have to enter a password in order to access them.

c) Not everyone has access to the internet, so the firm could miss out on potential customers if it only communicated through its website.

Page 40 — Electronic Communication

Q1 a) It only needs to be a short, informal message and it's **quicker** and **cheaper** than sending a letter.

b) Most business communications will need to be **longer** and presented more **formally** than a text message will allow.

Q2 Electronic notice boards are electronic **monitors** used for **displaying** up-to-date information in **public places**. They're often used in **railway stations**, **airports** or other places where up-to-the-minute information is important, as they can be quickly and easily updated electronically.

Q3 a) Supermarkets can use loyalty cards to collect data about a customer's **shopping habits**. A profile can be built up of each customer so that they can be **sent marketing** materials **aimed specifically** at things that will be of interest to them.

b) It is a more **efficient** method of marketing because time and materials **aren't wasted** sending something to people who are unlikely to be interested in it.

c) It is an **incentive** to encourage the customers to use their card.

Page 41 — Face-to-Face Meetings

Q1 A face-to-face meeting is **more personal** and would allow the colleagues to get **instant feedback** from each other both verbally and through body language. They also might find it easier to **discuss ideas** and **ask questions** — which can help reduce misunderstanding.

Q2 a) Silent communication may **contradict** a message that has been given verbally, causing **confusion** for the person receiving the message.

b) If the receiver looks like they **haven't understood** the message, it may lead to the sender **repeating** or **rephrasing** the message to make it **clearer**.

Q3 a) An appraisal is a meeting between a **manager** and **worker** to discuss the **worker's performance** over the year and to set targets for the coming year.

b) It can make it **easier** to discuss any personal issues or concerns the worker may have. It needs to be **two-way communication** so that the worker and manager can get **instant feedback** on their comments.

Q4 a) **Benefit** — it gives shareholders the opportunity to have a say in the running of the business.
Drawback — can be difficult to organise so that every person concerned can attend.

b) Various possible answers, e.g. They could send a **letter**, **report**, or **email**, or use the firm's **internet site** (e.g. they could have a password-protected part of the site that only shareholders can access).

Page 42 — Other Oral Communication

Q1 The customer will be able to **ask** the salesperson **questions** and get a **reply** straight away — unlike when ordering online where it might be hard to find answers to more specific questions. They might also be reluctant to order online using their credit/debit card because of **concerns** over **internet security**, e.g. identify theft.

Q2 a) Audio-conferencing allows **many people** in **different locations** to all **hear each other**. Video-conferencing allows them to **see each other** as well.

b) Benefit: It allows users to see each other's **body language**, so there's less chance of messages being misunderstood.
Drawback: The equipment required is much more **expensive**.

c) Many firms are now becoming multi-national (i.e. they have operations in more than one country). It is much **easier** and **cheaper** for them to hold meetings using teleconferencing than to get staff together in **one place**.

Q3 a) Since webinars can be interactive, the audience can **participate** by **typing comments** or **questions** for everyone to see — possibly a useful way for people to learn. However, since everybody needs to be logged on at a **particular time**, this may be **inconvenient** for some firms, and difficult to organise.

b) Since podcasts can be downloaded and viewed at **any time**, they are a **more flexible** way to provide training — different people can easily do the training at different times. But since podcasts are **not interactive**, people will not be able to ask questions — this could make the training **less effective**.

Page 43 — Visual Communication

Q1 Many possible answers, e.g.
• **Unique** — very different to other firm's trading names.
• **Catchy** — so it's easy to remember.
• **Fits in with firm's overall image**.

Q2 a) Logos usually contain a firm's **trading name** and an **image** which is used to sum up the **key messages** of the firm.

b) It's important that a logo is chosen which gives people the **right impression** of the firm as it will potentially be **seen by a lot of people** — it will probably feature on all the firm's products and written communications.

The Answers

Q3 It helps build an **identity** for the firm — it's important to get it right as adverts need to appeal to the **market groups** that the product is aimed at. If the adverts don't have the right tone or image, they won't persuade the target group to buy the product.

Q4 If a celebrity endorses a firm's products their **sales** will usually be **boosted**. The effect will be greater depending on how **popular** the celebrity is and how **connected** to the product they are (e.g. a TV chef endorsing pans).

Q5 a) Many possible answers, e.g.
"The logo helps **create an identity** to some extent — the boxes and trading name suggest they're a removal firm. But some of the **text isn't very clear** as it's upside down. Also one of the boxes appears to be **falling** which doesn't help create a **professional image** of the firm — it suggests this is the sort of removal firm that **doesn't care** too much about the goods they're moving. For these reasons, the logo may be more effective in creating a **negative impression** of the firm than a positive one."

b) Hints:
- **Graphics packages** can be really good for designing logos — you can apply all kinds of effects to text and graphics. (You could then **import** your logo into a word processor or DTP package to add the callouts.)
- The design of the logo is up to you, but it should reflect the **image** the company wants to convey.
- The company has a slightly jokey name, so they probably wouldn't want anything too serious. But they don't want to come across as sloppy, so something **neater** might be a good idea.
- For example, the boxes could be stacked carefully, with all the text the right way up in a tidy font. You could replace the 'T' with an arrow pointing upwards — this would tie in with the name.

Section Six — The Internet

Page 44 — How Businesses Use the Internet

Q1 **Internet** — A network of computers covering the whole world
World Wide Web — A huge collection of websites that can be viewed online
Web browser — A piece of computer software which allows you to view websites.

Q2 b) and d) should be ticked.

Q3 Many possible answers, e.g.
1. By providing technical support and software updates to customers.
2. By allowing customers to have online accounts which they can use to top up credit, pay bills, transfer money etc.
3. By displaying the answers to frequently-asked-questions (FAQs).

Q4 a) Publishing a catalogue on a website does **not require paper** — this may save money on printing costs. It also means that more **detailed information** can be included without a lot of extra paper being needed. Online catalogues can also be viewed by **anyone** with internet access, not just people that have a paper copy.

b) Guestbooks and online surveys allow businesses to collect **feedback** from their customers, and **improve** their products and services in response. This should help to attract more customers in the long term.

Page 45 — Business Websites — Benefits and Costs

Q1 Benefits of internet adverts include:
- They could include a **link** to Mandy's website, making it easy for people to navigate to it immediately.
- They can be **interactive** (e.g. an animation could be triggered when the user points their cursor at them) — this can help to catch people's attention.
- Mandy is advertising her **website**, so it makes sense to advertise online to reach people who **use the internet**.
- Mandy can **choose** to advertise on websites that would be popular with her **target market**.

Q2 a) Buying and selling goods and services on the internet.
b) Consumers can buy goods from the comfort of their home at a time that is suitable for them.

Q3 The internet can be accessed all over the world. So by advertising online, Purrfect Catz can reach people worldwide, or target markets in foreign countries with promotions.

Q4 Many possible answers, e.g.
Reduce costs: E-commerce businesses can sell direct from a warehouse, so they can save money that would otherwise be spent on rent for retail premises.
Increase costs: Extra staff may need to be employed to run and maintain the website, or existing staff may need expensive training.

Q5 Firms that sell online collect confidential information from their customers, e.g. credit card details — if their website isn't secure, unauthorised users may gain access and steal these details. The firm will **lose business**, could face costly **fines** under the Data Protection Act, and may get a reputation for being **untrustworthy**.

Page 46 — Websites and the Law

Q1 To comply with data protection law, businesses should make sure that part of their website is **encrypted** to protect payment data as it is collected. If they fail to do this, the business can be **fined** or the owners sent to **prison**.

Q2 Copyright laws mean that she can't use images, text or data from the existing web page on her website without **permission** from the **copyright holder** — if she does get permission she may have to pay a fee.

Q3 a) 1. They should be fit for purpose.
2. They should match their description.
3. They should be of a satisfactory quality.

b) Customers are legally entitled to an exchange or a replacement, which will cost the business and it could be more expensive for e-commerce firms as they may have to pay the costs of postage.

Q4 a) Selling when there is no face-to-face contact between buyer and seller.

b) 1. Companies must include clear information about themselves and their products.
2. Customers must receive written confirmation of any orders placed (could be by email).
3. Customers have a seven-day cooling off period where they can cancel their order without any penalty.

The Answers

Page 47 — Success of Business Websites

Q1 a) If a firm's website has successfully offered online customer support, this should result in fewer calls to the firm's telephone helpline.

b) If the telephone helpline is receiving fewer calls, the firm may be able to reduce costs by employing fewer people to answer the phones.

Q2 a), b) and d) should be ticked.

Q3 a) It's impossible to tell from this data whether the extra sales have come from the website or from a different part of the business.

b) E.g. FolderMart may be able to reduce the number of stores it operates.

Q4 E.g. Some firms may feel that they would benefit more by offering face-to-face contact with their customers — so a website wouldn't really help them.

Page 48 — Creating a Website

Q1 a) The website of a firm with a large budget will probably have more pages and information and is likely to have a slick, professional look to it. The website of a firm with a smaller budget is likely to be plainer with fewer animations and fancy graphics.

b) Setting up secure facilities for e-commerce can be expensive, so firms with small budgets need to be sure they'll earn this money back through internet sales.

Q2 A website containing too many graphics and animations may take too long to open for users with slow internet connections. Or a website might not be compatible with all web browsers. These could both lead to users visiting competitor websites instead, and the firm losing business.

Q3 a) To avoid embarrassing mistakes and to make sure that the website actually works. Also to make sure it is compatible with a variety of different browsers and hardware to make sure that as many users as possible can access the site.

b) Content needs to be kept up to date, and links need to be regularly checked to make sure they still work.

Q4 • You can be as creative as you like for this question — just make sure your webpage includes all the details of the dishes on the menu and their prices (in pounds, US dollars **and** Euros — try searching online for 'exchange rates').

• You'll also need to create **hyperlinks** to Wikipedia from the words in bold on the menu. Some of the foods may be listed under **different names** on Wikipedia, so make sure you're linking to the right pages.

• For example, go to www.wikipedia.org and search for 'celeriac' — you should go straight to the celeriac page. Copy the web address from this page and use it as the address for your hyperlink.

• You could write a bit of text to introduce the menu and give some details about the restaurant. If you just plonk the menu on the page, customers may feel you haven't made much of an effort. Make sure you've added a title to show that it's a menu, at least.

• Use a variety of text and paragraph formats, but don't go overboard — aim for a consistent, professional-looking page.

• Choose your colour scheme to suit the image of the business. Judging by the menu, the Chubby Goose is an upmarket restaurant, so hot pink and lime green may not be the best choices.

• The website's users are most likely to be adults, so make sure that the page design is appropriate.

• If you're including any graphics, remember that it's against the law for a business to copy images from other people's sites without permission.

Section Seven — Word Processing

Page 49 — Word Processors: Text Formatting

Q1 a) Ctrl+C, Ctrl+V, Ctrl+V, Ctrl+V...

b) i) Use an informal font like **Comic Sans MS** and make the text quite big, and a nice bright colour.

ii) A clear, formal font like **Times New Roman** or **Arial** in black.

iii) Something big and bold like **Impact**. Write it in CΛPITALS and make it an eye-catching colour.

Q2 a) Many possible answers, e.g.

1. The font used is **unclear**. It is an important message, so the font needs to be clear and easy to read.

2. The heading is much **smaller** than the text — to draw more attention to the message, it needs to be bigger and perhaps underlined too.

3. The text is too **faint**, which makes it hard to read — it needs to be darker, or an eye-catching colour.

b) Taking note of your answers to part a), I'm sure you've made your notice look like this:

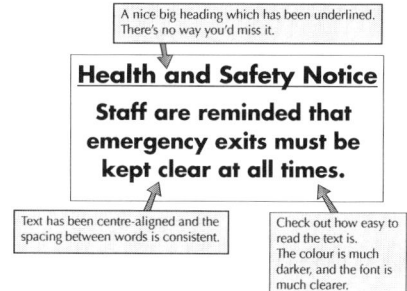

Q3 Your memo should look a bit like this:

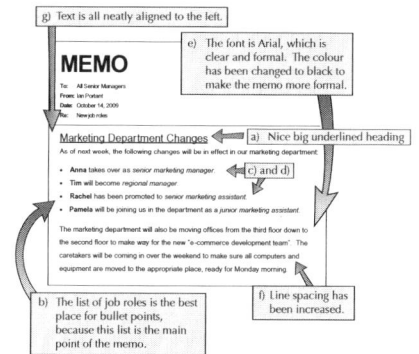

h) They make it **easier to read** and help point out the **key bits of information**. Making names bold or using italics can be useful for the reader, to **quickly look up a detail** in the memo.

Page 50 — Word Processors: Text and Graphics

Q1 a) You could use any person you like. I'm from Chester, so I chose a Roman:

b) Here's a few different types of callout you could use. Always make sure it's **clear** which bit of the picture they're pointing at.

The Answers

Q2 The first image is pretty straightforward, but you might have to do some dragging of wrap points to get the second image.

Q3 a) Text boxes keep chunks of text **separate** from the main text on the page, so that they can be **more easily moved around** without affecting the layout of the whole document.

b) It can make documents more **eye-catching** and **interesting** to look at.

Q4 a) They use pictures alongside text to make the advert more eye-catching.

b) I called mine '**FlyingPizza**'. Geddit? Flyer, pizza? Oh never mind.

c)-e) and g)-i)

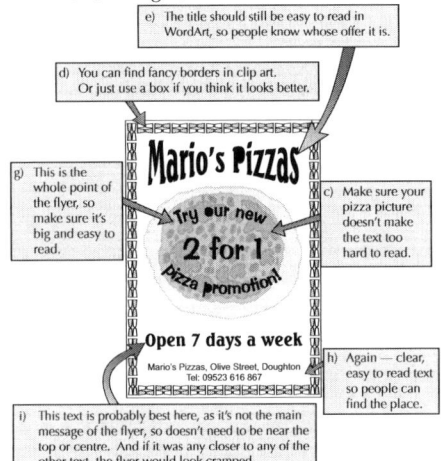

e) The title should still be easy to read in WordArt, so people know whose offer it is.

d) You can find fancy borders in clip art. Or just use a box if you think it looks better.

g) This is the whole point of the flyer, so make sure it's big and easy to read.

c) Make sure your pizza picture doesn't make the text too hard to read.

Mario's Pizzas
Try our new
2 for 1
pizza promotion!
Open 7 days a week
Mario's Pizzas, Olive Street, Doughton
Tel: 09523 616 867

h) Again — clear, easy to read text so people can find the place.

i) This text is probably best here, as it's not the main message of the flyer, so doesn't need to be near the top or centre. And if it was any closer to any of the other text, the flyer would look cramped.

f) It is a more eye-catching way to draw attention to the key information on the flyer, e.g. the name of the take-away.

Page 51 — Word Processors: Text and Graphics

Q1 a) It's a good idea to give your files a **meaningful** name, so you don't forget what the file is about. Something like '**HatTable**' would be suitable in this case.

b)-c)

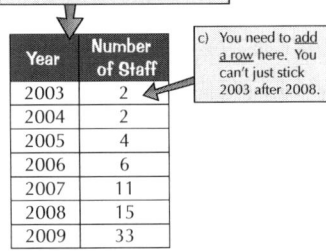

b) Here's the table. You can colour the background of the headings to make the table clearer.

c) You need to add a row here. You can't just stick 2003 after 2008.

Year	Number of Staff
2003	2
2004	2
2005	4
2006	6
2007	11
2008	15
2009	33

d) It makes the data easier to read.

Q2 a) 'Hats' seems as good as anything.

b)-d) Yours will look different depending on what hats you have chosen. You could use **callouts** or **arrows** to label your hats.

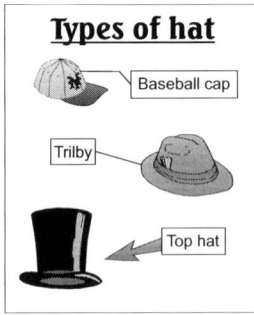

Types of hat
Baseball cap
Trilby
Top hat

Q3 a) It can make the text **easier** and **quicker** to **read**.

b) It can make columns look **tidier**.

c) **Big gaps** can appear between words.

Q4 Yours might look a little different, but it should look something like this:

The newsletter only needs a simple border. Anything more jazzy would make the page look too 'noisy' and might make the text more difficult to read.

White text on a black background or just simply underlining text makes the headings eye-catching.

Hats All Folks Newsletter
Number 27, January 2010

Record Heat brings Record Sales
We start another year here at Hats All Folks with excellent news – last year was our most successful year since we began trading way back in 2003. Our sales increased by 23% over 2008 and we had record profits of £3.4m. We were greatly helped by an unexpected surge in our sombrero sales during the summer. Celebrities were spotted wearing our sombreros and their pictures even featured in magazines such as "Hey Glossy" and "Trashtastic". It seems sombreros were the "must have" fashion item of 2009. Well done everyone on a really successful year, here's to 2010.

On the Up
Hats All Folks is now coming into its 8th year of trading. So we thought it'd be an appropriate time to remind everyone how far we've come.

The firm started from humble backgrounds in January 2003 selling Top Hats, specifically targeting them at people who wanted to appear taller. This was a roaring success and since then the firm has expanded its range of products. We now sell numerous types of hats including berets, Santa hats and trilbys. We've also increased the number of staff we have. The table below shows how much we have grown over the last 8 years, doubling our staff last year.

Year	Number of Staff
2003	2
2004	2
2005	4
2006	6
2007	11
2008	15
2009	33

This seems like the best place for the table, as this is where it's mentioned in the text.

It's great to have everyone on board.

Don't force justify your text, or it'll space these out to fill the whole line.

I found that size 16 font made the newsletter fill an A4 page quite nicely with just two columns. But this is a pretty big font — the newsletter might look better if there was more stuff on the page and a smaller font.

Page 52 — Word Processors: Business Letters

Q1 a) Templates are **standard documents** containing **pre-set formats** and layouts.

b) 1. It makes it **quicker** and **easier** to produce a letter, rather than starting from scratch each time.
2. It means all the letters from a firm have a **similar style**, creating a professional image.

Q2 Headers appear at the **top** of a page and footers at the **bottom of the page**. They appear on **every page of a document** and can be used to show page numbers, dates and company logos.

Q3 Many possible answers, e.g.
- Polite opening greeting of Dear Mr Raleway.
- Letter ended "Yours sincerely" with gap left for signature of the manager.
- Address of company put at top of letter.
- Fully blocked style
- Open punctuation
- Receiver's name and address
- Sender's name and position included at bottom of letter.

Q4 Hints:
- Using a **letter template** should help you make sure your letter has the correct layout.
- The question tells you to use a fully-blocked layout. This means that all the lines of your letter should start at the **left-hand margin** with the first line **not indented**.
- Remember, you're trying to **impress** the person reading this letter and convince them how professional you are. So starting the letter with "Alright mate" probably isn't the best idea. Use **formal language** like "Dear Sir/Madam" and "Yours sincerely".
- When you've finished your letter, **double-check** all the **spelling**, **punctuation** and **grammar**. If your letter's full of mistakes, it won't create a very **good impression** and you would be less likely to get the work placement.

Page 53 — Word Processors: Mail Merge

Q1 a) Inserting data from a data source into a word-processed document to produce a series of similar but customised documents.

b) Businesses can send out the **same letter** to lots of **different people**, but **personalised** with their name and address.

c) Many possible answers, e.g. It has become easier for firms to mass produce mailings targeted at individuals, so customers may receive more **junk mail**.

The Answers

Q2 a) **'ShareholderLetter'** worked for me.

b) This is how my letter turned out. I'm sure yours will be dead loads better.

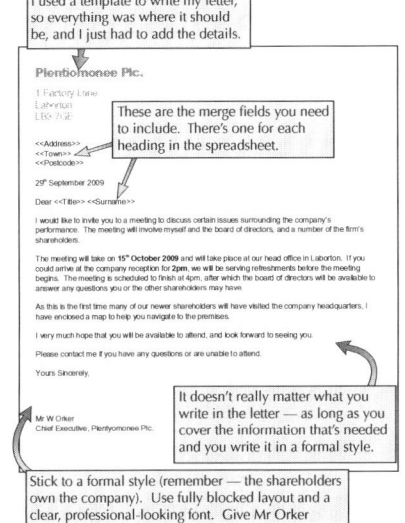

I used a template to write my letter, so everything was where it should be, and I just had to add the details.

These are the merge fields you need to include. There's one for each heading in the spreadsheet.

It doesn't really matter what you write in the letter — as long as you cover the information that's needed and you write it in a formal style.

Stick to a formal style (remember — the shareholders own the company). Use fully blocked layout and a clear, professional-looking font. Give Mr Orker plenty of space to scribble his signature.

c) After all the work in part b), actually performing the merge is pretty easy. You usually just press the button that says 'Perform mail merge' (or something like that). You should then be able to preview your six letters on screen and check for errors. Don't print all six letters out — think of the trees, man.

d) To check for **errors** — information might have gone into the **wrong fields** etc. It wouldn't look professional if the letter was sent out containing errors.

Section Eight — Spreadsheets

Page 54 — Spreadsheets

Q1 a) ii) should be ticked.

b) Rows are horizontal and columns are vertical.

Q2 a) It makes the data in the spreadsheet **clearer** — the **headings** and **key points** can be **highlighted**, to make it easier to pick out information.

b) Conditional formatting **automatically changes** the formatting of a cell based on the **data** in the cell, e.g. make all negative numbers red.

c) To keep sections of a spreadsheet **separate** from each other.

Q3 Spin the old book around 90 degrees and have a gander at what your spreadsheet should look like:

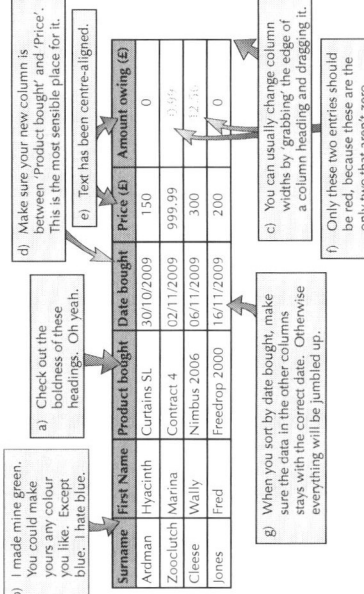

d) Make sure your new column is between 'Product bought' and 'Price'. This is the most sensible place for it.

e) Text has been centre-aligned.

c) You can usually change column widths by 'grabbing' the edge of a column heading and dragging it.

f) Only these two entries should be red, because these are the only two that aren't zero.

a) Check out the boldness of these headings. Oh yeah.

b) I made mine green. You could make yours any colour you like. Except blue. I hate blue.

g) When you sort by date bought, make sure the data in the other columns stays with the correct date. Otherwise everything will be jumbled up.

Surname	First Name	Product bought	Date bought	Price (£)	Amount owing (£)
Ardman	Hyacinth	Curtains SL	30/10/2009	150	0
Zooclutch	Marina	Contract 4	02/11/2009	999.99	0.99
Cleese	Wally	Nimbus 2006	06/11/2009	300	12.31
Jones	Fred	Freedrop 2000	16/11/2009	200	0

Page 55 — Spreadsheets: Using Formulas

Q1 a) **=C2+C3+C4+C5** (or =SUM(C2:C5))

b) i) **=C2*D2**

ii) Copying the formula into the other cells in the column. Either by **copying and pasting**, or **dragging the handle** in the corner of the cell down to E5.

Q2 a) B4 and E3

b) F1 and E3

c) G9 and E3

d) K14 and E3

Q3 a) Your spreadsheet should look something like this:

ii) **B8** is an **absolute** cell reference. When this formula's copied into other cells, it will still always reference cell B8

	A	B	C	D
1	Surname	First name	Hours worked per week	Gross wage
2	Goode	Phil	36	=C2*B8
3	Slave	Lisa	40	=C3*B8
4	Shirker	Kelly	24	=C4*B8
5	Slouch	Peter	1	=C5*B8
6	Total hours worked			
7				
8	Hourly wage:		£6	

i) This is now the cell that is referenced in the formulas for working out gross wage.

iii) If you've done it right, you should get these amounts:
Phil: £216
Lisa: £240
Kelly: £144
Peter: £6

b) Now that the spreadsheet uses absolute cell references, you only need to change £6 to £6.50 in **one cell**. The new gross wages should turn out to be:
Phil: £234
Lisa: £260
Kelly: £156
Peter: £6.50

Page 56 — Spreadsheets: Using Functions

Q1 a) i) =SUM(B2:B7) **or** =SUM(B2,B3,B4,B5,B6,B7)

ii) =AVERAGE(C2:C7) **or** =AVERAGE(C2,C3,C4,C5,C6,C7)

iii) =MAX(D2:D7) **or** =MAX(D2,D3,D4,D5,D6,D7)

b) It makes the function **quicker to enter** and it means you can **add new cells** to the middle of your range and the function will **automatically adjust** to include them.

Q2 a), c) and d)

a) A new row and column have been added to put these headings in.

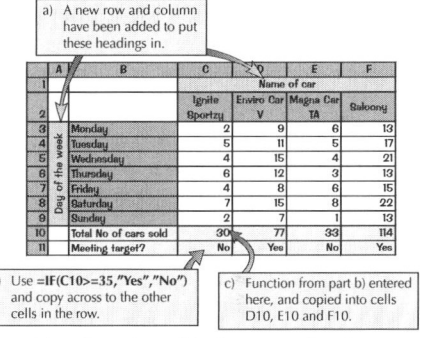

	A	B	C	D	E	F
1				Name of car		
2			Ignite Sportzy	Enviro Car V	Magna Car TA	Saloony
3		Monday	2	9	6	13
4		Tuesday	5	11	5	17
5		Wednesday	4	15	4	21
6		Thursday	6	12	3	13
7		Friday	4	8	6	15
8		Saturday	7	15	8	22
9		Sunday	2	7	1	13
10		Total No of cars sold	30	77	33	114
11		Meeting target?	No	Yes	No	Yes

d) Use =IF(C10>=35,"Yes","No") and copy across to the other cells in the row.

c) Function from part b) entered here, and copied into cells D10, E10 and F10.

b) If you've added rows and columns the same as in the diagram above, then your function should be: =SUM(C3:C9) **or** =SUM(C3,C4,C5,C6,C7,C8,C9)

Page 57 — Spreadsheets: Graphs and Charts

Q1 When you want to **compare quantities** of data that's **grouped into different categories**, e.g. number of people with different sized feet.

Q2 You might want to give your graph a heading and titles for the axes so it's easier for the reader to tell **what the graph is showing**. Changing the font type, size and colours of the bars can make a graph look **more attractive** — this can help show the data **more clearly**.

Q3 b) i)

The title should describe what the graph shows.

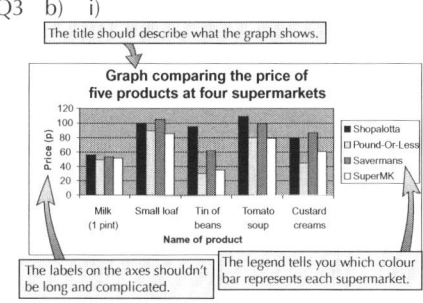

The labels on the axes shouldn't be long and complicated.

The legend tells you which colour bar represents each supermarket.

The Answers

ii)

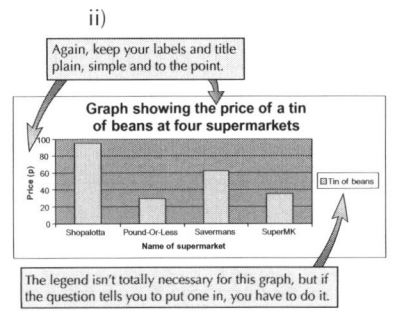

Again, keep your labels and title plain, simple and to the point.

Graph showing the price of a tin of beans at four supermarkets

The legend isn't totally necessary for this graph, but if the question tells you to put one in, you have to do it.

iii) and c)

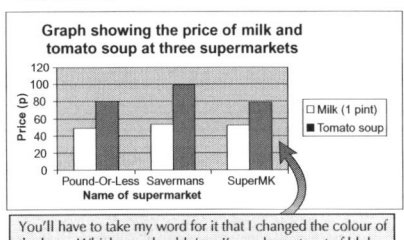

Graph showing the price of milk and tomato soup at three supermarkets

You'll have to take my word for it that I changed the colour of the bars. Which you should, 'cos I'm an honest sort of bloke.

Page 58 — Spreadsheets: Graphs and Charts

Q1 Line graph: When you want to show how the **quantity** of something **changes over time**.

Pie chart: When you want to show **proportions** of an overall total, e.g. the proportion of total sales contributed by each of a firm's products.

Q2 a) i)

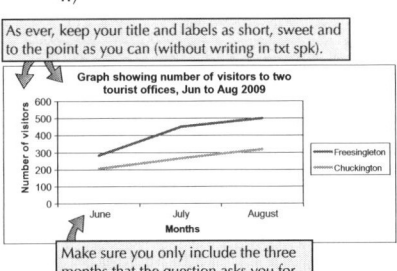

Graph showing number of visitors to three tourist information offices, Apr to Sep 2009

Make sure you include a title and a legend...

...as well as labels for the axes.

ii)

As ever, keep your title and labels as short, sweet and to the point as you can (without writing in txt spk).

Graph showing number of visitors to two tourist offices, Jun to Aug 2009

Make sure you only include the three months that the question asks you for.

b) i), ii), iii)

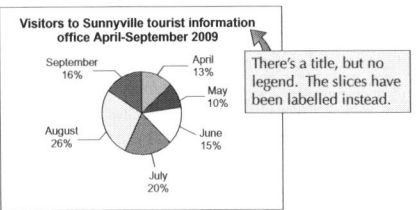

Visitors to Sunnyville tourist information office April-September 2009

There's a title, but no legend. The slices have been labelled instead.

iv)

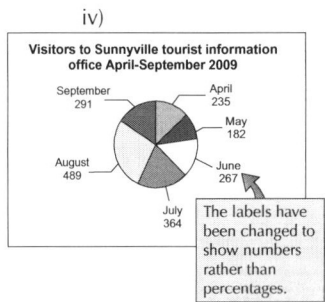

Visitors to Sunnyville tourist information office April-September 2009

The labels have been changed to show numbers rather than percentages.

Section Nine — Databases

Page 59 — Databases

Q1 a) A **field** is a **category of data** (e.g. name, telephone number, favourite colour). A **record** is a selection of **different pieces of information** about a particular person or thing. Each record usually contains a piece of information for each field. (For example, a record might contain information about one particular person's name, telephone number and favourite colour).

b) Suggested possible answers: date, currency, number.

Q2 a) Here's how your database table should end up looking:

First Name	Last Name	Job Title	Gender	Date of Birth	Emp. No.
Ivor	Plane	Pilot	M	26/09/1964	75167
Lisa	Spanner	Engineer	F	01/12/1980	76432
Holly	Copter	Pilot	F	25/12/1974	79429
Malcolm	Function	Accountant	M	14/03/1969	79621
Liz	Leader	Marketing Director	F	20/10/1977	79643

b) A key field is a field that is **different in every record** — it means that no two records can be the same (i.e. the key field ensures every record is **unique**).

c) 'Employee No.' would be the best choice, since it will be **different for every employee**. (Different employees may have the same names, job titles and dates of birth.)

Q3 a) A flat-file database contains all its data in **one** table. Relational databases store data in **more than one** table — records in different tables can be **linked** using their key fields.

b) Many possible answers, e.g. Relational databases are an **efficient** way to store lots of information about things which are **different**, but which are **linked** in some way. (For example, a shop might have separate tables recording details of its products and suppliers, but these tables can be linked to show which supplier provides which product.)

Page 60 — Databases: Data Input Forms

Q1 a) Data input forms are supposed to make entering data more **user-friendly**, and reduce the risk of errors. If a form isn't clear, users may be confused and enter the **wrong information**.

b) An input mask defines what **format** data in that field should take. For example, for a date you could use the input mask ##/##/####, where each # represents a digit from 0 to 9.

c) Displaying the input mask makes it **clear** to the user what the format of the data should be, making **mistakes less likely**. You can also often edit how the mask is displayed. E.g. you could display **dd/mm/yyyy** to show that 2 digits are required for the day and month, but 4 digits are needed for the year.

Q2 a) Here's how my table looked:

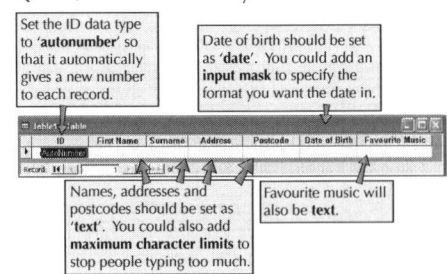

Set the ID data type to '**autonumber**' so that it automatically gives a new number to each record.

Date of birth should be set as '**date**'. You could add an **input mask** to specify the format you want the date in.

Names, addresses and postcodes should be set as '**text**'. You could also add **maximum character limits** to stop people typing too much.

Favourite music will also be **text**.

b) In my software, I have to change the data type to '**Lookup Wizard**' to create the drop down menu. The wizard takes you through step-by-step and allows you to type in all the options you want to include in the menu.

The Answers

c) I used the Form Wizard, and I ended up with the following:

First Name	
Surname	
Address	
Postcode	
Date of Birth	
Favourite Music	▼

Record: I◄ ◄ |

Pop
Rock
Disco

Here's the drop down menu.

d) Here's my finished table (I gave it a better name too).

ID	First Name	Surname	Address	Postcode	Date of Birth	Favourite Music
1	Justin	Timberline	5 Riverside Lane	CR8 2YM	13/05/1982	Pop
2	Calvin	Harrison	28 Didcot Road	RF2 8TW	26/03/1963	Rock
3	Oscar	Osbawn	8 Rockcliffe Avenue	BA6 9TS	26/03/1963	Rock
4	Kylie	Minoglie	33 Lucky Lane	LO3 9CO	18/09/1974	Pop
5	Kenny	East	13 Rappin Close	BL6 3NG	27/01/1967	Disco

Record: I◄ ◄ | 6 ►|►I► of 6

Page 61 — Databases: Simple Queries and Sorting

Q1 Sorting records involves putting data **into a particular order**. Filtering involves **picking out** data that you want using search criteria.

Q2 a) iv)
b) iii)
c) i)
d) ii)

Q3 a) A wildcard search allows you to search for **part of** a record — e.g. you might want to search for people whose last names **begin** with M. An asterisk (*) is used for wildcard searches.

b) i) All records where the entry in that field starts with "A".
ii) All records where the entry in that field ends in "my".
iii) All records where the entry in that field starts with "P" and ends in "s".

Q4 a) There are lots of ways you can do this. In my database package, I can click somewhere in the Surname field and click on the 'Sort Ascending' button on the toolbar. Or I can right-click on the surname field and select the 'Sort Ascending' option from the pop-up menu. However you do it, make sure the records end up sorted into alphabetical order by surname.

b) Your search results should be:
i) [Search for **"Taylor"** in the Surname field.]
• Mr Ashley Taylor
• Mrs Meera Taylor

ii) [Search for **"Twinton"** in the Town field.]
• Mr John Pillbox
• Ms Sarah Lampington
• Miss Julia Plankton
• Dr Jamal Singh
• Mr Peter Ringout
• Miss Janet Nowak
• Ms Dora Brown
• Mr Saul Yodel

iii) [Search for **Like "J*"** in the First Name field.]
• Mr John Pillbox
• Miss Julia Plankton
• Dr Jamal Singh
• Miss Janet Nowak

iv) [Search for **Not "Ms"** (or **<> "Ms"**) in the Title field.]
• Mr John Pillbox
• Miss Julia Plankton
• Mr Harold Brown
• Mr Ashley Taylor
• Dr Jamal Singh
• Mrs Lucia Gently
• Mrs Meera Taylor
• Mr Peter Ringout
• Mrs Hilda Kohl
• Miss Janet Nowak
• Mr Saul Yodel

v) [Search for **"Brown"** in the Surname field _and_ **"Y"** in the Payment Received? field.]
• Ms Dora Brown

vi) [Search for **"Like P*"** in the Surname field _and_ **"Y"** in the New Student? field.]
• Mr John Pillbox

Page 62 — Databases: Simple Queries and Sorting

Q1 a) Fred Bucket
b) Fred Bucket
c) Ivor Short
d) Jack Barge and Frank Mooney

Page 63 — Databases: Producing Reports

Q1 a) **a table** and **a query** should be ticked
b) If the report has been made using a **query** rather than a table, only those records that satisfy certain criteria can be **filtered out** and shown in the report. Reports can also present data in **various forms** (e.g. in tables, in **columns**, as a **graph**), and formatted in various ways (e.g. using different **colours**, **fonts** etc.). This means that the data can be shown in a way that is as **clear** and **useful** as possible.
c) Headers and footers are printed at the **top** and **bottom** of each page of a report. This means, for example, that the title and page numbers can be made to appear on **every page**, which can be useful on long reports.

Q2 a) Search for Not **"Twinton"** (or **<> "Twinton"**) in the Town field. Choose **Sort Ascending** in the Surname field. Choose to show only the **Title**, **First Name**, **Surname** and **Town** fields. You should find records for these students:
• Mr Harold Brown, Borginton
• Ms Karen Faber, Borginton
• Mrs Lucia Gently, Lutington
• Mrs Hilda Kohl, Billsburgh
• Mr Ashley Taylor, Mapsbury
• Mrs Meera Taylor, Mapsbury

b) Using a **Wizard** should make this question fairly easy. You'll need to use your query from part a) as the **data source** for the report — the Wizard will talk you through the rest.

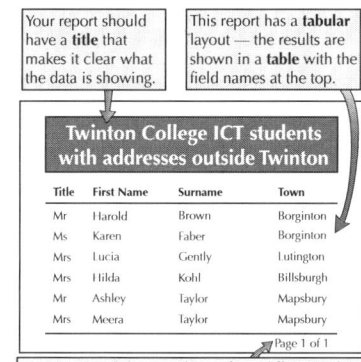

Your report should have a **title** that makes it clear what the data is showing.

This report has a **tabular** layout — the results are shown in a **table** with the field names at the top.

Twinton College ICT students with addresses outside Twinton

Title	First Name	Surname	Town
Mr	Harold	Brown	Borginton
Ms	Karen	Faber	Borginton
Mrs	Lucia	Gently	Lutington
Mrs	Hilda	Kohl	Billsburgh
Mr	Ashley	Taylor	Mapsbury
Mrs	Meera	Taylor	Mapsbury

Page 1 of 1

Report wizards let you choose from different **colour schemes**, **styles** and **options**. I've included a **footer** which includes the page number. Exciting stuff.

Q3 a) Search for **"Twinton"** in the Town field _and_ **"Y"** in the New Student? field. Choose **Sort Descending** in the Date of Birth field. You should find records for these students:
• Mr John Pillbox, 02/05/1987
• Ms Sarah Lampington, 13/12/1985
• Ms Dora Brown, 16/10/1982
• Dr Jamal Singh, 20/07/1980
• Mr Peter Ringout, 17/03/1974

The Answers

b) Designing your own report from scratch is trickier than using a Wizard. Choose the **query** from **part a)** as your data source, and use the report design view to lay your report out the way you want it. To display the data, you'll need to create **text boxes** and **link** them to fields in the query. Use **labels** to create titles and headings, and experiment with the colour and shape options. Here's what I managed:

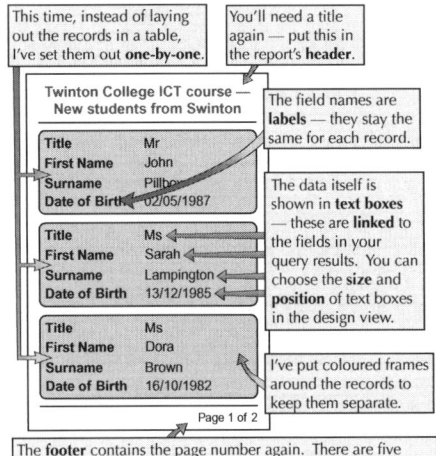

This time, instead of laying out the records in a table, I've set them out **one-by-one**.

You'll need a title again — put this in the report's **header**.

The field names are **labels** — they stay the same for each record.

The data itself is shown in **text boxes** — these are **linked** to the fields in your query results. You can choose the **size** and **position** of text boxes in the design view.

I've put coloured frames around the records to keep them separate.

The **footer** contains the page number again. There are five query results — the last two would be shown on the next page.

Q4 a) Search for "**N**" in the Payment Received? field. Your query should return the names **and full addresses** of these students:
- Mr John Pillbox
- Miss Julia Plankton
- Mr Harold Brown
- Dr Jamal Singh
- Mr Peter Ringout
- Mr Saul Yodel

b) The letter's already been written, so you just have to insert the **merge fields** and a couple of **dates**. Open the word processor file and go to the mail merge options. Choose your query from part a) as the **data source** for the mail merge, and **insert** merge fields in the places marked in the letter.

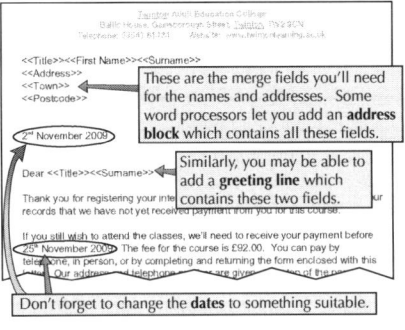

These are the merge fields you'll need for the names and addresses. Some word processors let you add an **address block** which contains all these fields.

Similarly, you may be able to add a **greeting line** which contains these two fields.

Don't forget to change the **dates** to something suitable.

You should have created six letters addressed to the people you found in part a). The first one should look something like this:

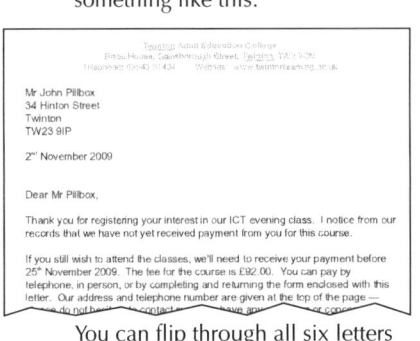

You can flip through all six letters on-screen to make sure the details are correct — if they're not, go back and tinker till you've got it right.

Section Ten — Other Software Applications

Page 64 — Graphics: Creating Images

Q1 Most graphics packages will have **tools** that allow you to make the shapes listed here — just investigate the **toolbar**. You'll probably have to draw the 'blob' shape **freehand**, and **edit a rectangle** or an **oval** to make the speech bubble. But you're up to that challenge, I can tell.

Q2 The important thing to get right here is the **width** of the lines. This can usually be changed by selecting the object and choosing the line width you want from a **drop down menu**. Also, there's usually a box for you to type in the line width you want, if it's not listed in the drop down menu.

Q3 Hints:
- It's usually pretty easy to change the fill colour of an object — in most graphic packages, you just select an object and pick a colour from a **palette**.
- It gets a bit trickier when you want to shade an object using more than one colour. Although again, your graphics package should have a tool that lets you do this. You might even be able to choose a **pre-set pattern** or shading from a menu.
- You should be able to change the **style of shading**. Part c) uses a '**linear** fountain fill' (that's what my graphics package calls it anyway) but part e) uses a '**radial** fountain fill' (a circular shading pattern basically). There should be some options in your fill tool for you to change this.

- You can also change the **line style** of your selected object from the toolbar — instead of having a continuous line you could change it so that it's **dashed** or **dotted**.

Q4 The image has become **stretched** — this can be avoided by making sure the **proportions** are kept the same when the image is re-sized.

Q5 a) Your picture will probably look quite different, but you'll still need to do some of the same things:

You might have to **rotate** the top hat so it fits neatly on the cat's head.

You can **change the order** of your two graphics (usually by right-clicking on one of them). Bring the top hat forward, so it's in front of the cat. This makes it look more like the cat is wearing the hat.

You'll need two different clip art graphics for this question, so you'll have to do some **re-sizing** so that they fit together nicely.

b) Again, your answer will look different if you've used different clip art, but here's a few hints:

You can take off the robot's head using the crop tool in your graphics package.

Try to find two graphics that are facing the same way — it makes it easier to put them together.

Rotate and re-size the robot's head until it fits perfectly. My robot's head neatly covered up the man's head. You might need to take the man's head off with the crop tool — yuk.

When you're resizing a graphic, remember to keep the proportions the same, otherwise you could end up having a man with a very squashed robot's head.

Page 65 — Graphics: Manipulating Images

Q1 a) **Removing** parts of a picture which you don't want.

b) Your answer should look like this:

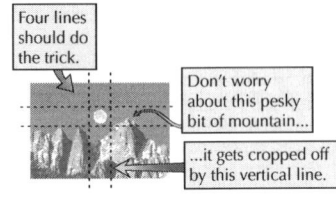

Four lines should do the trick.

Don't worry about this pesky bit of mountain...

...it gets cropped off by this vertical line.

The Answers

c) Your pictures should look something like this:

i)

Your picture will probably have a little bit of the table left around the edges — most standard cropping tools only allow you to crop in straight lines.

ii)

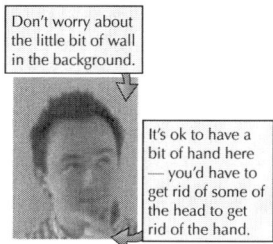

Don't worry about the little bit of wall in the background.

It's ok to have a bit of hand here — you'd have to get rid of some of the head to get rid of the hand.

iii)

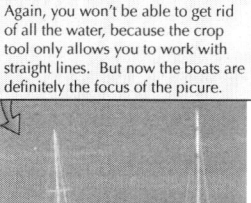

Again, you won't be able to get rid of all the water, because the crop tool only allows you to work with straight lines. But now the boats are definitely the focus of the picure.

Q2 Many possible answers, e.g.
1. **Copy and paste** the image into the document.
2. **Insert** the graphic using the **menus** on the word-processing software (e.g. 'Insert image from file').

Q3 Your answer might look a bit like this:

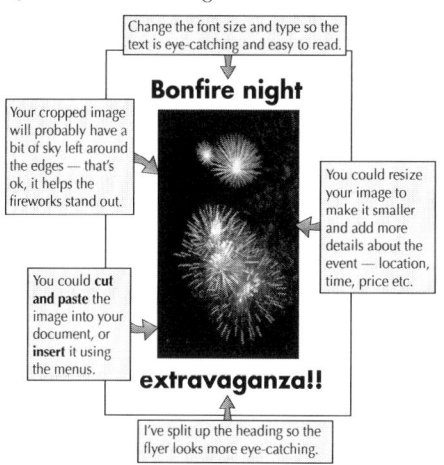

Change the font size and type so the text is eye-catching and easy to read.

Bonfire night

Your cropped image will probably have a bit of sky left around the edges — that's ok, it helps the fireworks stand out.

You could resize your image to make it smaller and add more details about the event — location, time, price etc.

You could **cut and paste** the image into your document, or **insert** it using the menus.

extravaganza!!

I've split up the heading so the flyer looks more eye-catching.

Q4 If it is only a simple diagram, it may be **quicker** and **easier** to use word-processing software. Especially if the user is unfamiliar with graphics software.

Page 66 — Presentation Software

Q1 Visual communication can help **support** the information given **verbally**. It can also help keep the **audience's interest** and **summarise the key ideas** being talked about.

Q2 **Lines and borders**, **transitions between slides** and **animation effects** should be ticked.

Q3 E.g.
a)

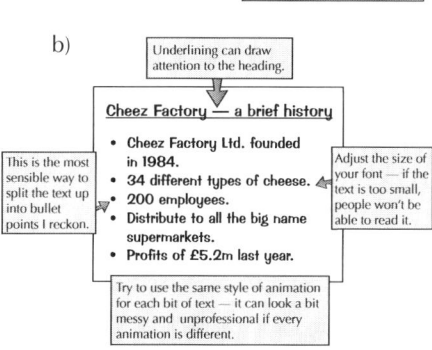

I just used plain text, but you could use WordArt if you wanted to jazz up the title a bit.

Put the text in the centre of the slide — it'd look well weird stuck up at the top.

An Introduction to Cheez Factory Ltd.

Make sure the heading is nice and big so it's easy to read.

b)

Underlining can draw attention to the heading.

Cheez Factory — a brief history

- Cheez Factory Ltd. founded in 1984.
- 34 different types of cheese.
- 200 employees.
- Distribute to all the big name supermarkets.
- Profits of £5.2m last year.

This is the most sensible way to split the text up into bullet points I reckon.

Adjust the size of your font — if the text is too small, people won't be able to read it.

Try to use the same style of animation for each bit of text — it can look a bit messy and unprofessional if every animation is different.

c)

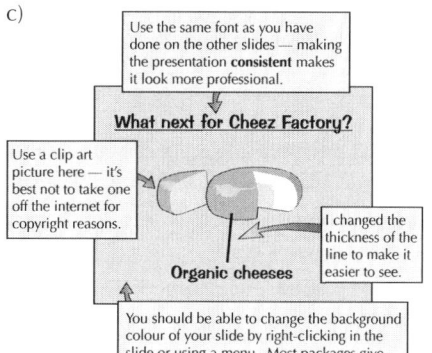

Use the same font as you have done on the other slides — making the presentation **consistent** makes it look more professional.

What next for Cheez Factory?

Use a clip art picture here — it's best not to take one off the internet for copyright reasons.

Organic cheeses

I changed the thickness of the line to make it easier to see.

You should be able to change the background colour of your slide by right-clicking in the slide or using a menu. Most packages give you the option of applying the background to all the other slides at the same time.

Q4 Your changes to the presentation might look something like this:

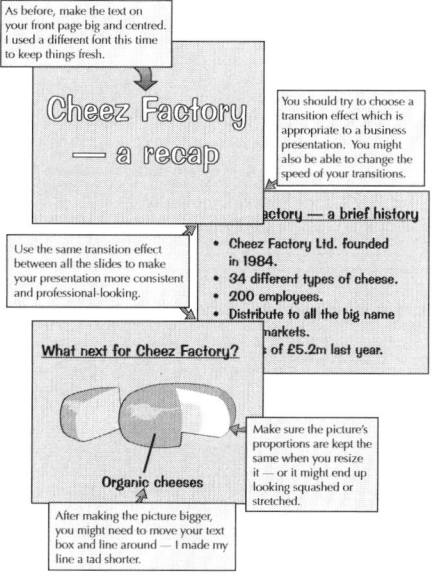

As before, make the text on your front page big and centred. I used a different font this time to keep things fresh.

Cheez Factory — a recap

You should try to choose a transition effect which is appropriate to a business presentation. You might also be able to change the speed of your transitions.

Use the same transition effect between all the slides to make your presentation more consistent and professional-looking.

...actory — a brief history
- Cheez Factory Ltd. founded in 1984.
- 34 different types of cheese.
- 200 employees.
- Distribute to all the big name ...markets.
- ...s of £5.2m last year.

What next for Cheez Factory?

Organic cheeses

Make sure the picture's proportions are kept the same when you resize it — or it might end up looking squashed or stretched.

After making the picture bigger, you might need to move your text box and line around — I made my line a tad shorter.

Page 67 — Presentations

Q1 Many possible answers, e.g.
1. **Reduce** the **amount of information** on the slide to make it easier to read.
2. Use **bullet points** to draw attention to the key points.

Q2 Many possible answers, e.g.
1. Can experience **technical problems**.
2. Equipment more **expensive** to buy.

Q3 a) The presentation is for a large number of people, so a slideshow projected onto a **large screen** will be the best way to present this information so that **everyone can see** it. The meeting will also be quite **formal** so a slideshow would be the most **professional** and appropriate way to present his information.

b) So that people in the presentation have their **own copy** of the information which they can make their own **notes** on or **refer back** to at a later date.

Q4 Hints:
- This question is a really good chance to practise all your presentation-making skills.
- First, **save your presentation** with a suitable name — I called mine "FaveTVShow". It's best to save it at the **beginning** and then **regularly** as you go along — so you don't lose everything if your computer decides to crash or something.
- Try to keep transitions, animation effects, background colour and fonts the same throughout your whole presentation — this **consistency** helps give your slideshow a **definite style**.

The Answers

- Don't put **too much information** on each slide — and use **bullet points** to break text up so it's easier to read.
- Add **notes** to your presentation that will remind you of things you want to talk about as each slide comes up. My presentation software lets me add notes underneath the slides as I'm making them.
- The question also asks you to print off two copies of your presentation — on my package I selected "print preview" from the file menu — this lets me change how many slides I wanted to print on each page and whether I want my notes included too. Your presentation software will probably have the same, or a similar, option.

Page 68 — Web-Authoring Software

Q1 It helps create a more **professional** image of the firm if every page is of a similar style. A consistent layout may also make it **easier** for customers to **navigate** their way around the website — this may help the firm get repeat visitors to their website.

Q2 **Frames:** These allow different parts of a web page to work independently, e.g. a menu bar at the side could remain fixed while the main section of a website is scrolled through.
Hyperlinks: These are clickable links that will take you to a page either on the same website or a different one.
Borders and lines: These can be used to help break up a page — making it easier to read.

Q3 **Benefit:** The images look much better than low-resolution images.
Drawback: They can take a long time to download.

Q4 Hints:
- This question really tests your web-authoring skills and creativity. You could pick a destination you already know quite a bit about, or do some internet **research** on one you are interested in.
- There's no right or wrong answer with this question — just make sure you include all of the features listed in the question. Also, think about the **audience** you are aiming your website at — is it appropriate for them?
- Your website should have a **consistent** layout and format to help create a professional image — it'll also make it easier for people to find their way around.

- Think about the **fonts** you want to use and whether they're appropriate for the website's theme — it's ok to use a couple of font types, but it's best not to have loads of different ones — it'll make the page look messy.
- Think about what **colour scheme** you want for your website — what sort of colours are "holiday" colours? Try to keep the colour scheme the same on all three pages, to keep a consistent theme.
- Try not to have lots of text on your website — people might get bored of reading if there is too much information. Use **bullet points** and **short paragraphs** to present your key points. You could also use **borders** and **lines** to separate different parts of your pages too — to make them easier to read.
- You'll need to create **hyperlinks** on each of the pages to make your website easy to navigate — you could give your hyperlinks titles, e.g. "Things to do".

Page 69 — DTP and Evaluating Software

Q1 Both allow the user to combine text and graphics on a page, using similar tools. However, desktop publishing packages are **frame-based**. This means that all the objects on the page (pictures, blocks of text, etc.) are contained in individual frames, allowing them to be moved around freely.

Q2 a) The drawing tools in a word processor are quite **basic** — you can draw lines and simple shapes, but it's hard to produce more complex pictures. Using these tools would probably make the picture look **unprofessional** to the customers who read the newsletter.
b) Graphics packages have **more sophisticated** drawing tools that she could use to make the picture look more **professional**. She may also be able to use this software to **edit a clip art picture**, rather than drawing a boat from scratch. She could then import her picture into the word processor.

Q3 Spreadsheets allow a business to organise its numerical data into easy-to-read **tables**. Formulas and functions in the spreadsheet can then be used by the business to quickly perform **calculations**. It's also possible to produce **charts** and **graphs** to represent the data in a visual way — making it easier for people within the business to interpret the data.

Q4 a) Possible answers:
- If there's a **problem** with the **internet connection**, the hospital may not be able to access information it urgently needs.
- Web-based software stores data on internet servers. This may make patients' private medical records **vulnerable to hackers** all over the world.

b) Possible answer:
Web-based software stores data on internet servers. This means authorised users can access the **same data** from **different locations**, making it easier for team members to view and edit the same files.

Assessment Skills

Page 70 — Controlled Assessment

Q1 These are the features you should tick:
- Company name ('Filmic Cinema')
- Strap line ('Bringing you the best in film since 1953')
- Images (any of the photos, or the clip art in the logo)
- Contact details (the cinema's address and telephone number)
- Menus (the main menu on the left, or the 'Films' menus on the right)
- Clear space (e.g. there's a white space in the bottom-left corner)
- Hyperlinks (e.g. the film titles on the right of the screen)
- Bullet points (e.g. the list of film titles on the right of the screen)

Q2 a) There's not a 'right' answer to this question (although it would be difficult to argue that the logo looks 'high-tech'). I'd say that the logo makes the business look **traditional**, **stylish** and **enthusiastic about film**.

b) Here's how I'd explain my answers: "The cinema's logo includes a picture of a projector and some film reel — this emphasises the **traditional** aspects of the business (it's been around since 1953). It also suggests they have a genuine **interest in cinema**. But the font used for the text is bold and modern, which shows that the business isn't stuck in the past — they've probably chosen the images in the logo to convey a 'classic' **style**."

Q3 - The font used for 'Kids' Club Films' has a '**handwritten**' look. It seems **childish** compared to the rest of the site — it may help to create the impression that children are welcome at the cinema.

- A clear sans-serif font is used for 'Weekdays at 11.30am' (it's the same font that's used for most of the text on the page). It looks **straightforward** and **unfussy** — this creates an image of reliability, which is useful when giving out **factual information** like times and dates.

Q4 Hints:
- There are lots of websites you could choose — you could pick a few websites that you use regularly, e.g. a news site, or the site of your favourite football team or band.
- Try to use a few **different-looking** websites, with a range of **different features**.
- Write down the **features** that are used on each website — use the features list from Q1 to help you.
- Pick a few features and think about them in more **detail** — why have they been used, and do they work well?

Page 71 — Controlled Assessment

Q1 a) The basic message is that Takeaway Maths is a business that **offers maths tuition** to school students. The flyer also suggests that the business is **good** at what it does.

b) The flyer is aimed at **parents** of school-age children. This is made clear by the phrase, 'your child's grades' in the second paragraph.

c) Takeaway Maths will be hoping to **persuade parents** to become their customers (i.e. pay the business to give maths tuition to their children).

Q2 a) Overall, the flyer is a **good choice** of medium. It's being delivered to houses on estates **near schools**, so it should reach a lot of parents with school-age children. The flyers are delivered through people's doors, so there's a good chance that people will **see** them.
On the downside, a lot of the flyers will probably be **thrown away** without being read, and some will be delivered to people who **aren't interested** in the service (e.g. single people with no children). These flyers will be **wasted**, and some people will be **annoyed** with the firm for sending them junk mail.

b) There are plenty of other media that could be used. For example:
- A **printed advertisement**: With a few tweaks, the flyer could be published as a printed advertisement — this would save the business printing thousands of copies themselves. Local newspapers or school magazines may be good places to advertise, since they would be read by a large number of parents.
- A **notice**: The message could be put up on a notice board (e.g. in local shops and libraries). This would be a cheap method of advertising, but the notice would probably be ignored by most people passing by.
- A **radio advert**: The business could record an oral message to be broadcast on a local radio station. This may be heard by a large number of people, but many of them would live a long way from the business. Radio advertising time is expensive, so Takeaway Maths would have to think carefully about whether this was right for them.

Q3 a) **Technical jargon**: The flyer mentions 'trigonometry', 'calculus' and 'non-linear dynamical systems'.
Spelling/punctuation errors:
- In the box under the company name, 'professional' is misspelt as 'proffesional'.
- In the first paragraph, 'Its' should read 'It's'.
- In the first paragraph, 'lose' is misspelt as 'loose'.

Irrelevant information:
In the third paragraph, we don't need to know how Chris Jennings raised the money to start the business.
We also don't need to know what subject he studied at university.
Exaggerated or untrue statements:
The 'guarantee' that students' grades will increase after four weeks sounds a little over-confident.

b) - The maths jargon **isn't necessary** to the message, and may **put people off**, especially since the company claims to be sympathetic to people who struggle with maths.
- Errors always make business messages look **unprofessional** (especially when 'professional' is misspelt). These mistakes will make parents **doubt** whether the tutors know what they're talking about.

- Irrelevant information makes the message more **cluttered**, and can be **confusing**. In this case, it may damage the image of the business, since it sounds as if Chris Jennings is boasting about his achievements.
- Businesses need to be careful not to exaggerate their claims — it may lead people to **doubt their honesty**.

Q4 • The photos on the page don't add much meaning to the flyer, but they do **break up the text** and make it more **visually appealing**.
- The photo at the top conveys an **informal** image, and ties in with the first paragraph of text.
- The middle photo isn't really relevant — the message wouldn't be changed if it was removed.
- The photo of Chris Jennings at the bottom is probably supposed to add a **personal** touch, but some readers may think he's just got a **massive ego**.
- The graph in the background of the flyer is just a 'maths' object that doesn't add any meaning. It also makes the text **harder to read**, as the lines and labels on the graph overlap with it.

Q5 a) This comes down to your opinion. Think about your answers to the previous questions and the general **tone** of the writing — how do these features add up to give an overall impression? I'd say the flyer is **friendly**, a little bit **smug**, and slightly **unprofessional**. But that's just my opinion.

b) Judging by the tone and the content, the business is probably aiming to present a **professional**, **reliable** and **friendly** image.

Q6 There are plenty of improvements that could be made — look again at the answers to questions 3, 4 and 5 for ideas.
For example:
- The tone of the writing could be made less boastful.
- The errors should be corrected.
- The photo of Chris Jennings could be one that looks less smug.
- The graph in the background should be removed.
- The font and colour used in the speech bubbles makes the text hard to read — this could be changed to make it clearer.

The Answers

Q7 Hints:
- You'll probably be able to find some business documents lying around your house, e.g. adverts in magazines, flyers for local takeaways or mail-order catalogues.
- You need to try to work out **what message** each document is trying to communicate, decide **how effective** it is and then **suggest improvements** to the document. Simples.

Page 72 — Exam Marks

Q1 Anita has only said that teleconferencing uses telecommunication devices to hold meetings. She hasn't mentioned that the people in the meetings are located in **different places** (which is an important point). Rachel's answer includes both these points, so she gets two marks.

Q2 a) The question is asking for a **short definition** of 'remote storage' and **one** example. You could cross out the whole first sentence, the phrase 'so that it can be retrieved even if the main office burns down' and all of the last sentence — Jo would still get 2 marks.
   b) If Jo writes this much more than she needs to for every question, she'll run out of time in the exam.

Q3 **1 mark out of 2**. Gethin has given two disadvantages, but that's not what the question asked for. To get both marks, he needed to **explain** why one problem with portable storage devices might be a disadvantage to the business **in the case study**. E.g. 'Portable storage devices can be lost or stolen. Customers' private financial data could fall into the wrong hands if this happened.'

Page 73 — Exam Marks

Q1 a) **4 marks out of 4** — Ellen has **identified** several strengths and weaknesses of each medium (cost, security, accessibility and convenience). She has also **applied** them to the scenario from the question — for example, she uses the fact that Horsley's are currently sending out thousands of letters each month to show that the cost of paper statements will be high.

b) **6 marks out of 6**, because Ellen has written a **well-structured**, **well-written** answer that shows **good judgement** that is **relevant to the situation** in the question. Ellen has identified the key issues that are likely to be important to Horsley's and has weighed up how suitable each medium is for addressing these issues. Each paragraph suggests that she feels the website would be a better option, which leads up to her overall judgment in the final paragraph. She also says that it would be best if customers were given some choice, which shows that she has considered the needs of the customers as well as the business.

Pages 74-76 — Sample Exam Questions

Q1 a) An open-plan office is a **large room** containing **many desks**.
   b) Having the whole team in one room makes it easier for them to **communicate**. This is important to Reyah's team, since they work closely together.
   c) i) Flexitime means that staff can **choose when** they work, as long as they still work a set amount of hours **in total**. Some flexitime workers have to work during fixed **core hours**.
      ii) Teleworking means that staff use ICT to work from places **outside the office** (usually from home). Work can be sent and received through an **internet connection**.
   d) Possible answer:
   Flexitime and teleworking give staff **control** over their working week. This makes it easier to fit their jobs around their families and hobbies, which may improve their motivation and productivity. However, Reyah's team members may end up working in **different places** at **different times**. This would break up the team's face-to-face communication, which may reduce their efficiency and creativity. Since it's important for her staff to work closely together, it would be better for Reyah not to change the current working practices of the team.

Q2 a) Suggested answers:
   - A **keyboard** could be used for entering customers' names and addresses into the database.
   - A **mouse** could be used for selecting options from multiple-choice lists (e.g. type of credit card).

b) Suggested answers:
   Allowing customers to input their own details could **reduce the number of staff** needed to take phone calls and input the data from paper forms. This would **reduce** the company's **wage bill**. It could also **reduce the number of errors** in the database. If customers enter their details directly, there is **less chance** of **mistakes** being made due to information being **misheard** on the phone, or **misread** due to unclear handwriting. The data form could include **validation checks** so that customers would not be able to submit the form without all the necessary data.

c) Suggested answers:
   - **Firewall** software could help to block external users from accessing the data. It works by monitoring the users who are moving through a network, and denying access to anyone who doesn't have authorisation.
   - **Encryption software** converts data into a coded form, making it impossible to read without the key that decodes it. Only authorised users have the key, so the coded data would be useless to hackers and other intruders.

Q3 a) i) A salary is a **fixed** amount of pay that employees receive each year, regardless of their output. It's usually paid in monthly instalments.
      ii) Commission is an **extra** payment given to sales staff — the more items they sell, the more commission they receive. If their basic salary is low, but commission rates are high, staff will be motivated to sell more windows so that they can earn a good rate of pay.

b) i) • A **CV** contains details of a candidate's skills, qualifications and experience. This information is usually split into standard **sections**.
   • An **application form** asks candidates for **specific** information that's **relevant to the job** — each candidate is asked for the same information.

The Answers

ii) Linda would need to **compare** these documents to the **job description** and **person specification** — the standard formats of CVs and application forms make it easier to do this. This would allow her to judge which candidates are **most suited** to the job.

c) The job will involve talking to potential customers — this will require **confidence** and good **verbal** communication skills. These things can't be tested in a written application, so Linda may prefer to meet them for a face-to-face interview to see how well they perform.

Q4 a) i) E-commerce is the buying and selling of goods and services **over the internet**.

ii) Possible answer:
E-commerce is available 24 hours a day — this means that customers can place orders when it's **convenient** to them, not just during shop opening hours.

b) Suggested answers:
- Setting up and maintaining a website can be **expensive**. This may increase the firm's **costs**.
- The company's **reputation** will suffer if there are problems with the website, e.g. if customer data is lost or stolen from their website.

c) Possible points to include in your answer:
- The company produces electrical equipment, so some customers may have **complicated** questions to ask about the products — the responses may involve **detailed** information.
- The telephone uses **oral** communication — this means that customers can explain their problems and receive **immediate feedback**. If the customer doesn't understand something that's been said, they can ask a question and the advisor can answer it straight away — this can avoid confusion.
- This is more difficult with email — the customer will send their question, and then have to **wait** for a response. If the email messages are unclear, it may take several messages (and a long time) to clear up the confusion.

- Email is a **written** medium — this means that the information in a message can be read **as many times as needed**, which could be useful if it contains detailed instructions. With a telephone call, the customer may forget important information and have to call back — this is **inefficient** for the business, since they would be paying staff to give out the same information twice.
- On the other hand, the customer could follow the instructions step-by-step whilst on the phone, which many people would find easier than following written instructions.
- With email, it may be possible for the company to produce **standard** email answers to common questions, which would save them time and resources — with a phone line, staff would have to talk different customers through the same information time and time again.
- You'll need to make a **judgement** about how well email would compare to the phone line. Whatever you conclude, make sure you back it up with a well-structured argument that's relevant to the case study.

Q5 a) i) It has been designed to be **comfortable** and **easy to use**.

ii) Suggested answers:
- If staff feel comfortable it may improve their **motivation** which might increase the **productivity** of the firm.
- Ergonomic workstations can **reduce injuries**, e.g. back pain — the number of days that the firm's staff take off due to **illness** could be reduced, saving the firm money.

b) Suggested answers:
- Employees should take **regular breaks** from their computer, e.g. taking a walk or exercising their fingers. This can help **prevent injuries**, e.g. repetitive strain injury and eye strain.
- They should follow instructions on the **correct** way to **sit** — this could help avoid **back pain**.
- They should adjust the **brightness** and **position** of their screen to meet their needs — this could help reduce the risk of **eye strain**.

Q6 a) A task that is carried our **regularly**, which is often the **same** each time, e.g. filing, inputting data.

b) i) Induction training **prepares** a new member of staff for their job and aims to make them feel **welcome**. They may receive a **tour** of the firm, training on their new role and information on **company rules**.

ii) Possible points to include in your answer:
- The workers need to be trained in how to use software that has been **specifically** made for the firm. **In-house training** might prepare them better for this, as the firm will have a better **knowledge** of the software than an outside organisation would, e.g. a training college.
- It is **cheaper** for the firm to have in-house training as the new employees will be working and learning at the same time.
- However, if the training is done in-house, there is a possibility that the employees might pick up **bad working practices** from current employees.

c) Suggested answers:
- He could use **presentation software** to create a **slideshow** to accompany his speech. The slides could contain the **key information** from his talk — this might help keep the interest of the listeners, who otherwise might find it hard to **pay attention** if he is just reading out information from a piece of paper.
- Will could make his presentation **shorter**. This reduces the chance of people becoming **bored** and 'switching off'. If he has a lot of information to give to the employees, **two shorter presentations** may be more effective than one long one.

ISBN 978 1 84762 411 6

9 781847 624116

BCAA41